D1490779

God Off-Broadway

The Blackfriars Theatre of New York

Matthew Powell, O.P.

Introduction by
Robert Anderson

The Scarecrow Press, Inc.
Lanham, Md., & London
1998

SCARECROW PRESS, INC.

Published in the United States of America
by Scarecrow Press, Inc.
4720 Boston Way
Lanham, Maryland 20706

4 Pleydell Gardens
Kent CT20 2DN, England

This book is a major revision of the author's doctoral dissertation, "The Blackfriars Theatre of New York: An Experiment in Catholic Theatre," University of Wisconsin–Madison, 1984.

British Library Cataloguing in Publication Information Available

Library of Congress Cataloging-in-Publication Data

Powell, Matthew, O.P.
  God off-Broadway : the Blackfriars Theatre of New York / Matthew Powell.
    p.   cm.
  Includes bibliographical references and index.
  ISBN 0-8108-3417-0 (alk. paper)
  1. Blackfriars Guild. New York Chapter—History. 2. Theater—New York (State)—New York—History—20th century. I. Title.
PN2297.B57P68   1998
792'.09747'1—dc21 97-29111

ISBN 0-8108-3417-0 (cloth : alk. paper)

Dedicated to

FATHER URBAN E. NAGLE, O.P.

(1905–1965)

whose vision and creativity made Blackfriars possible.

CONTENTS

ACKNOWLEDGMENTS

The author would like to thank the following people for their valuable assistance in the preparation of this book: Robert Anderson, playwright; Dr. James Moy, professor of theatre at the University of Wisconsin at Madison; Jane Jackson, director of archives at Providence College; Robert Booth, associate director and projects manager of the Providence College Publications Office; the late Professor Frank Hanley, Providence College; and Elizabeth Brady and Michael Sablone, typists.

INTRODUCTION
by Robert Anderson

The production of my play, *Come Marching Home*, at the Blackfriars Guild Theatre in New York in 1946 was a major turning point in my life. It was my first production, on or off Broadway.

I had written the play aboard the newest ship in the fleet, the battle cruiser *Alaska*, during our shakedown cruise in the Atlantic. After shakedown, we were headed for the Pacific. Though I had written plays in college, I was desperate to leave a "last play" behind . . . "to be remembered by!!!" (Strangely, it was about a naval officer returning from war, not setting out for war.)

I had received my M.A. from Harvard in 1940, and in 1942 had passed my oral exams for the Ph.D the night before I was commissioned in the Navy. (I have often thought they passed me on the assumption that I would not be coming back.)

And I did not want to come back to write a thesis and become a Ph.D. I wanted to be a playwright. But, being a "belt and suspenders man," I had felt that I should have some other way of earning a living . . . just in case.

Though I had acted in college productions and had sometimes thought of being an actor, a lovely woman who had directed these productions had persuaded me that I was a better playwright than an actor. Needless to say, I married her in 1940.

On my return from the shakedown cruise and before heading off to the Pacific, I left *Come Marching Home* with my wife, who submitted it to the Army-Navy National Theatre Conference play contest for servicemen.

I was on the oldest ship in the fleet, the battleship *Texas*, either at Iwo Jima or Okinawa (it was more than fifty years ago and I have forgotten) when I learned that I had won the play contest, and that if I managed to return home, I would come marching home a playwright and not a Ph.D. candidate.

On the strength of winning the award and a Rockefeller Grant, I had landed a top play agent, Audrey Wood, who also represented Tennessee Williams. I was released from active duty at the end of 1945, and in 1946 Miss Wood had arranged for a production of *Come Marching Home* at the Blackfriars Guild Theatre.

As you will read in Father Powell's fascinating account, the Blackfriars Guild Theatre was founded by Father Urban Nagle and Father Thomas Carey, two Dominican priests who loved the theatre, but not the kind of theatre being produced on Broadway. If I had known this at the time, I might have had second thoughts, because I thought I had written a play *for* Broadway. It was about a naval officer who had come home full of idealism, only to be confronted by the ugliness of politics when he decided to run for office in his small city.

There is an irony which readers of Father Powell's book will discover. Though Father Urban and Father Carey had in mind starting a Catholic theatre in reaction to Broadway theatre, the Blackfriars became one of the first, if not *the* first Off-Broadway theatre where young actors and actresses flocked to try their wings, with dreams of making it big *on* Broadway. To name but a few, there were Geraldine Page, Eileen Heckart, Patricia Neal, Anthony Franciosa and Darren McGavin. Only one play originally done at Blackfriars moved to Broadway, but many were published and were performed in college and regional theatres throughout the country.

Dozens of fine professional actors (who were paid nothing) showed up for auditions for the director, Dennis Gurney, and me. Rehearsals went smoothly without any problems, and after rehearsals, Father Nagle, Dennis Gurney and I enjoyed repairing to a nearby pub to discuss the day's progress.

But I was sleepless the night of the opening. Many playwrights do not attend their openings. The strain is too great. So much is at stake.

Starting with *Come Marching Home*, I have always attended. For me it's part of the learning process. A play is not a play until it has an audience. The play exists somewhere between the stage and the audience. There can be many different kinds of audiences. Hence, different plays on different nights.

When I first caught sight of one particular audience at Blackfriars, I almost went into shock. I almost turned and ran down the stairs and out into the night. The audience was made up entirely of nuns! And, of course in 1946, all in black habits.

I found a chair and sat, with my mind running through my play, wondering if there was anything that would embarrass the dear sisters. The play was partly about the returning officer and his wife trying to have a child. My mind went blank. Father Nagle explained to me that nuns came from a cross section of society and they would be a great audience. They were.

About ten years later, when I wrote the screenplay for *The Nun's Story*, which starred Audrey Hepburn, my romance with nuns continued. In Rome I became very fond of the nuns bustling around on the set, working to make Audrey's costume and performance authentic. She loved them, and they loved her. Riding in a taxi, I would wave at a cluster of nuns floating down a street, only to be admonished by my director, Fred Zinnemann, "You don't wave at nuns." I did, remembering how kind their "sisters" had been that night at the Blackfriars Guild Theatre.

The leading New York critics came, which they did not always do for later Off-Broadway productions. They were kind, perhaps because I was a veteran. They called me "promising," which was all I was at that time. But the Blackfriars Guild experience paved the way for a summer theatre production of a different play in 1951, a regional theatre production of another play in 1952, and finally in 1953, my "arrival" on Broadway with *Tea and Sympathy*, which changed my life.

I do not know if Father Nagle and Father Carey ever saw *Tea and Sympathy*. I don't think it was a play they would have wanted in their theatre (except they would have approved of the theme: "we have to give each other more than tea and sympathy.") But I think they would have been pleased that one of "their playwrights" had made it, and might not have made it without his baptism at Blackfriars.

CHAPTER 1

BACKGROUND OF THE BLACKFRIARS: CHURCH AND THEATRE IN AMERICA

In 1940 two Catholic priests of the Dominican Order rented a small auditorium on West Fifty-seventh Street in New York. Thus began the Blackfriars Theatre, also known as the Blackfriars Guild of New York, a part of the larger national Blackfriars Guild movement. This experiment in Catholic theatre would last for thirty-two years.

Blackfriars was one of the very few attempts by a religious group to conduct a professional-level theatre, the only professional-level theatre ever conducted by a Catholic organization in the United States and the first religious theatre ever tried in New York City.[1]

In addition, Blackfriars assumed a pioneering role in Off-Broadway theatre. Blackfriars began advertising itself as the "oldest continuous Off-Broadway theatre" in 1960.[2] It is difficult to verify this claim since it depends on what one means by Off-Broadway. Howard Greenberger in *The Off-Broadway Experience* states that Off-Broadway began in 1914 with the Washington Square Players.[3] Stuart W. Little, on the other hand, writes in *Off-Broadway: The Prophetic Theatre* that Off-Broadway really began in 1952 with Circle-in-the-Square's production of *Summer and Smoke*.[4] Julia S. Price in her history, *The Off-Broadway Theatre*, includes Blackfriars.[5] However, Robert Louis Hobbs in his dissertation, "Off-Broadway: The Early Years" mentions Blackfriars as one of the early pioneers of Off-Broadway along with Equity Theatre

Library, the Provincetown Playhouse, the American Negro Theatre and the American Repertory Theatre.[6] Whatever the definition of Off-Broadway and whenever it began, Blackfriars participated in its early history.

Blackfriars provided an opportunity for many important artists to get their start in the theatre. Robert Anderson, who later wrote *Tea and Sympathy*, *You Know I Can't Hear You When the Water's Running* and *I Never Sang for My Father*, had his first New York production at Blackfriars. Actors who got their "breaks" in Blackfriars productions include Geraldine Page, Eileen Heckart, Patricia Neal, Anthony Franciosa, Darren McGavin and Shelley Berman. Producer Elizabeth McCann began by working backstage at Blackfriars.

Lastly, and perhaps most importantly, Blackfriars attempted to synthesize theatre and religion, to resolve a centuries old conflict between the theatre and the Church. Although not always in agreement, the staff of Blackfriars reflected on the relationship between theatre and religion, God and the stage.

The Blackfriars Theatre was very much a product of American Catholicism in the first half of the twentieth century. Blackfriars, however, did not exist in a vacuum but had to find its place in the milieu of the New York theatre. In addition Blackfriars had an official relationship to the Dominican Order since all the priests who worked with the theatre belonged to that Order and ultimate authority rested with the Provincial of St. Joseph's Province of the Dominican Friars.

The Dominican Order: A Brief History

Father Urban Nagle, O.P., and Father Thomas Carey, O.P., the founders of Blackfriars, and other priests who worked with the theatre belonged to the Order of Preachers more popularly known as the Dominicans.[7] The Dominicans are an international order of priests and brothers founded in 1216 in Toulouse, France by a Spanish priest, Saint Domingo (Dominic) de Guzman.[8] He founded the order in a time when all other religious orders (whose members were often well educated) were strictly cloistered and monastic while the diocesan or secular clergy (not members of religious orders) were often poorly educated. In his efforts to combat the heresies of his day, Saint Dominic saw the need for a well educated and mobile group of priests who would be both contemplative and active. They would be dedicated to preaching and teaching the Catholic faith. Their rule allowed for greater flexibility in order to achieve their goals. It was, in fact, the first religious order not to require manual labor of its members, but instead to require study.

Early Dominicans engaged in both street corner preaching on the one hand and teaching in the great university centers -- Bologna, Paris, Oxford -- on the other. In 1221, five years after their founding, the Dominicans established themselves at Oxford University.[9] The Dominicans adapted their ministerial techniques to individual situations. The thirteenth century preacher Blessed James of Voragine, for example, used musicians, jugglers and acrobats to attract an audience for his sermons.[10]

In its 750 years the Order produced such diverse men as Albert the Great, bishop and natural scientist; Thomas Aquinas, who synthesized Aristotelian philosophy and Christianity and who probably influenced Catholic thought more than any other theologian; Fra Angelico, Renaissance fresco painter; Girolamo Savonarola, Florentine political and religious reformer burned at the stake for heresy and schism; and Bartolome de Las Casas, champion of the rights of Indians in the Americas.

In England the Dominicans came to be known as the "Blackfriars" because of the black mantles or "cappas" which they wore over their white habits whenever they went outside or when they were preaching. The Dominicans established a priory in London in 1224 and moved to another location in 1275. This later priory also became known as "Blackfriars." Henry VIII confiscated the property and expelled the friars in 1538.[11] He gave various parts of the priory complex to his friends; the Master of Revels, for example, used one section for costume and property storage. The refectory remained unused until 1576 when Richard Farrant, Master of the Children of Windsor Chapel, adapted the hall as a theatre. This theatre, known of course as "Blackfriars," was the first private theatre in England. Children's companies and later James Burbage used this and a subsequent theatre in the same building. William Shakespeare and Ben Jonson were associated with this theatre. This explains, then, why Fathers Nagle and Carey chose the name "Blackfriars" for their Catholic theatre venture.

In 1510 the Dominicans came to the New World and in 1551 they founded the first university in the Americas, the University of Lima.[12]

However, the friars did not come to the United States until 1804 when
three English friars and one American-born friar arrived from Belgium
to establish an American province. Later the friars grew to over 1200
members in the United States and occupied themselves with
preaching, teaching, writing and parochial work.

The establishment of a theatre by Father Nagle and Father Carey
was quite in keeping with the history and tradition of their Order.

The American Catholic Cultural Situation

The American Catholic Church at the time of the founding of
Blackfriars was still, in many ways, an immigrant church. At the end of
the Revolutionary War Catholics numbered fewer than 40,000 in the
United States. By the beginning of the First World War that number
had grown to over fifteen million.[13] Great waves of German, Italian,
Irish, Polish and Lithuanian immigrants poured into the United States,
the vast majority being Roman Catholics. Not only strangers to
America, its customs, and its language, they also practiced a religion
that most Americans considered strange. John Cogley, in his book
Catholic America, writes, "American Catholics have always been
different from their fellow citizens. In the beginning the outstanding
thing about them was that they were not Protestants, in a nation
where almost everyone else was. . . ."[14]

The prevalent anti-Catholicism of Protestant America also greatly
influenced the Catholic cultural situation. Cogley states,

> Anti-Catholicism has been called America's most abiding prejudice. In
> early New England it went unquestioned. It was rooted in the theological
> narrowness then dominant in the Western world, and, perhaps more
> powerfully, in the history of the Mother country.[15]

Their position as immigrants and still later as the children of
immigrants, coupled with the anti-Catholicism of their fellow
Americans made it more difficult for Catholic immigrants to assimilate.
They became insular and defensive and, at times, suspicious of the
Protestant establishment. The nation's public institutions were
nominally "nonsectarian," but "nonsectarian" often meant that they
did not favor one branch of Protestantism over another. The
Protestant Orphan Society of New York, for example, was publicly

charged with the care of all the orphans of the city of New York (most of them Catholic) and it systematically instructed the children in the tenets of Protestantism.[16] Legislation required reading from the King James version of the Bible in public schools. Many of the powerful social and benevolent fraternal organizations excluded Catholics from their memberships, "and as often as not they used their life-or-death influence to deprive non-Protestants of job opportunities and other means of social advancement."[17]

Catholics responded by setting up their own institutions. Catholic educational institutions, ranging from kindergartens to graduate schools, became one of the chief works of the Catholic Church in America. Catholic cemeteries, hospitals, orphanages, settlement houses and homes for the aged came to number in the hundreds.

> American Catholicism has maintained its own press and publishing houses, fraternal organizations, hospitals and social-service agencies, professional and academic societies. Unlike their co-religionists on the Continent, they held off from establishing sectarian labor unions, and political parties, but in almost every other area of life they produced counterparts of the dominant social structure--a Catholic war veterans association, Catholic Boy Scouts, a Catholic organization dedicated to the prevention of cruelty to animals, even a society of Catholic philatelists.[18]

This resulted in a "ghetto culture" that departed markedly from Archbishop John Carroll's notion of Catholics integrated into American life. It became, in time, the best organized and most powerful of the nation's subcultures -- "a source of both alienation and enrichment for those born within it and an object of bafflement and uneasiness for others."[19]

> The world of ghetto Catholicism had its own best-selling authors, prominent lecturers and in-house controversialists who were known in ghetto circles from coast to coast. It was frequently divided by lively arguments over theological and philosophical issues which were barely comprehensible to persons outside the Church -- such as intramural disputes as to whether Graham Greene's fictional Scobie was "saved," for example, or whether abortion was permissible in cases of ectopic pregnancy, or whether Catholic Action without a bishop's "mandate" was authentic. It dispensed highly sought-after sectarian awards and

medals, maintained its own *Who's Who*, and cast up its own celebrities, who sometimes went altogether unnoticed elsewhere but were lionized within the walls.[20]

It is understandable, then, that many Catholics felt the need for a distinctively Catholic theatre as opposed to or in addition to the secular commercial and community theatres.

The Reaction of the Catholic Church to the Theatre in America Up to the Founding Of Blackfriars

The Catholic Church in colonial America, a small religious minority, struggled to survive in a Protestant country. Preoccupied with other concerns, the Church had little or no cognizance of the theatre until the early nineteenth century. Then came the first of several important developments.

Conciliar Decrees Concerning the Theatre

In 1810 Archbishop John Carroll and the four other American bishops published a decree admonishing priests to attempt in their sermons and private instructions to draw the laity away "from a fondness for and an inordinate love of plays and those entertainments which they cannot attend without danger, such as frequently going to the theatre, indulging in dances, etc."[21] The document seemed to be directed only at entertainments which Catholics could not attend "without danger" and did not appear to forbid all attendance at the theatre nor did it seem to have been taken that way.

In 1866 the Second Plenary Council of Baltimore, attended by all American bishops, prohibited clergy from attending "plays, shows and dances." It also urged pastors to "prudently turn the faithful away from theatres and plays, especially those which are known to be evil or full of danger."[22] However, this directive specifically warned pastors against prohibition of all attendance at theatres, acknowledging the laity's "evangelical liberty." The document however did, at least, imply the prevalent sinful nature of most plays.

Father James Hinnen, canon lawyer for the Catholic Diocese of Madison, stated that the bishops most likely enacted the regulation in response to some abuse. He went on to say that the prohibition against priests attending the theatre was probably widely ignored from the beginning.[23] In fact, there are records of bishops complaining about their clergy attending plays, but this writer could find no indication of a priest ever being punished for doing so. Father Hinnen was also unaware of any such clerical censure. On the contrary, some priests seem to have been avid theatre-goers. The diary (1886-1893) of Father Richard L. Burtsell, himself a canon lawyer of the Archdiocese of New York, lists the many plays that he and his priest-friends openly attended and indicates that they were quite knowledgeable about the theatre.[24]

In 1885 the Third Plenary Council of Baltimore reiterated its prohibitions that priests stay away from the theatre and added horse racing to the list of forbidden entertainments. The Council made no attempt to forbid these of the laity. The document stated that things which may be suitable for the laity are not necessarily suitable for the clergy.[25]

As late as 1936, a priest wrote a letter to the question and answer column of the *Homiletic and Pastoral Review*:

> One of my fellow-religious maintains that by Canon Law all clerics and religious are forbidden to attend theatres. Now, *theatre-going seems to be quite general among priests in this country*, and I should like to know if Canon Law forbids it or how the law is interpreted here. By theatre-going I mean to respectable productions.[26]

The columnist gave a conservative answer, perhaps because his response would be published. He referred to the decree of the Third Council of Baltimore and pointed out that the decree made no distinction between good and bad shows; "all are prohibited to priests." This stricter regulation for the American Church contrasted markedly with the canon law for the whole Church which merely forbade priests to be present at entertainments which were "unbecoming" or at which people might be scandalized to see a priest. The columnist went on to infer that not all bishops enforced the regulations -- "Some dioceses in the United States do not forbid priests to attend respectable theatres."

It is also important to note that the questioner stated in 1936 that theatre-going seemed to be quite general among priests in this country and that the questioner, himself a priest, was unaware of any prohibition against attendance at the theatre.

While these conciliar decrees may have been widely ignored and unenforced, their very existence does indicate that American Catholic leaders felt that inherent dangers existed in the theatre and that the theatre must be approached with caution.

The Catholic Actors Guild

In 1899 an Episcopal priest, the Reverend Walter Edmund Bentley, founded the Actors Church Alliance (A.C.A.), an inter-denominational organization to minister to the religious needs of Protestant, Catholic and Jewish actors. There was no official Catholic representation, but Catholic priests such as Father Thomas Leo Ducey served in an unofficial capacity as chaplains to the organization's Catholic members.[27]

In 1912 Father Bentley asked John Cardinal Farley, archbishop of New York, to join officially in the work being done by the A.C.A. In response Cardinal Farley appointed Father John Talbot Smith as the official Catholic representative on the A.C.A.'s national council. The national council later requested that Father Smith form a separate branch for Catholics. This provided the beginning for the Catholic Actors Guild. Exactly why a separate denominational branch was formed is unclear.[28] Perhaps the A.C.A. felt unable to minister to the special needs of Catholics. In May 1913, *America* had urged the formation of a Catholic organization in New York similar to the Catholic Stage Guild in England because it felt that there was a need for a society to uplift the stage and minister to Catholic theatre professionals.[29] The *America* editorial may have been the spur to the formation of the Catholic Actors Guild.

At any rate, on March 31, 1914, Father Smith met with a group of twenty-five actors at the Astor Hotel to form the Catholic Actors Guild of America.[30] They elected Emmet Corrigan as their first president. They formally inaugurated the C.A.G. on June 8, 1914. The organization stated its purpose as the care for the spiritual welfare of people in the theatrical profession. In November of the same year, Cardinal Farley received a delegation of C.A.G. members, including George M. Cohan. In February, 1915, Farley gave his official approbation, designated Saint Malachy's Church on West 49th Street as the actors' church and appointed Father Joseph F. Delaney as chaplain. The cardinal, however, was cautious in his approval. He told the actors: "I do not want you stage folk to develop the idea that the Catholic Church now formally approves of things on the stage. The Church deals with you as individuals and as Roman Catholics."[31]

Farley's attitude contrasted with that of Patrick Cardinal Hayes, who became archbishop in 1919. Hayes gave unreserved support to the Guild and said: "A movement like the Catholic Actors Guild will do more for the dramatic and moral betterment of the stage than condemnation and censorship."[32] Later he told members of the Guild,

> I am in sympathy with the people of the stage. They are often maligned; they are blamed for conditions for which they are not responsible. If conditions on the stage are not what they should be, it is the community and not the stagefolk who are to blame.[33]

Having taken note of Cardinal Hayes' friendly attitude toward the theatre, Father Smith brought forth his pet project and dream -- a professional Catholic theatre. On October 19, 1919, Smith urged the C.A.G., whose membership now numbered over 500, to consider his proposal:

> Broadway will not produce real Catholic plays. Let us produce them ourselves. We have the actors, the authors, the producers. Why don't we go ahead, put up a theatre and produce plays? I guarantee it will be filled every night of the year.[34]

Cardinal Hayes responded with interest and approval. Unfortunately Father Smith's death shortly thereafter from cancer put a halt to the idea.

The Catholic Actors Guild prospered, however. It arranged for Masses at hours to fit actors' schedules, provided financial assistance to needy actors, engaged in other welfare activities and arranged for an annual spiritual retreat. The organization still exists.

The Catholic Theatre Movement

> The amusement question is one of the most vital problems of our country, for as marvels of stage realism are multiplied they are being used mainly to degrade and corrupt the public mind in every city and every land. It is evident that the Church must use the means at her

command to curb a mighty influence that will otherwise undermine her sacred teaching.[35]

This was the call of Eliza O'Brien Lummis, a prominent Catholic laywoman, for the formation of an organization to keep a moral watch on the New York commercial theatre. In the spring of 1912, with the approval of Archbishop John Farley of New York, she founded the Catholic Theatre Movement (C.T.M.). Early plans for the organization called for an inter-denominational venture with a positive approach. As part of this positive approach Lummis proposed a religiously-oriented, but non-sectarian professional theatre which would compete successfully for patronage with the "objectionable" commercial fare. She named the proposed theatre the Excelsior.

Between June and October 1912 the concept of the Catholic Theatre Movement appears to have changed. Lummis no longer mentioned an interdenominational effort. The Excelsior Theatre was shelved and the focal point of Miss Lummis' endeavor began to shift from Catholic production to Catholic criticism. The statement of purpose in October read

> to unite our Catholic laity in demanding purer ideals for the drama; to provide for Catholic supervision of plays; to give substance to Catholic protest; to open a way to the public demonstration of Catholic principles through the medium of the stage.[36]

It is not clear why this change took place, though hierarchical pressure may have been involved. Whatever the reason for the change, the departure from the original ideal can be seen in the four functions of the organization listed by Mrs. Lummis just a year later:

1. Refuse to support unapproved plays.
2. Offer demand and support for wholesome plays.
3. Make more public assertion of Christian principles.
4. Gain the press in the endeavor.[37]

The primary activity of the C.T.M. became its "White List" of approved plays which it began issuing in 1914.[38] The standards for being included on the White List were clear: all moral, none artistic.

> "Indeed, the narrow interpretations subsequently applied by Catholic Theatre Movement reviewers pushed aside a great deal of artistic

achievement to spare Catholic ears from a few 'damns' and an off-color remark."[39]

One gained membership in the movement by signing a promise card that stated that the member would avoid "improper" plays and entertainments and attempt to influence others to do the same. Movement officials encouraged members to support the police in their attempts to keep theatres clean, to be on the lookout for cases about which the police should be notified, and to avoid denunciation of specific plays, which would only be free advertising. This last part caused the C.T.M. to believe that its approach was positive.

The Catholic Theatre Movement prospered for a while but the decade of the 1930's marked the beginning of its end. The depression caused financial problems for it, and a gradual loss of interest created difficulty in securing reviewers. The ratings were often the product of one or two untrained people. "Since its reviewers for the most part paid too much attention to superficiality and too little to dramatic content, the Movement could find little sympathy even among Catholic playgoers."[40] Statements by the Catholic Actors Guild, the Blackfriars Guild and the National Catholic Theatre Conference that disavowed censorship and a negative approach further isolated the group. C.T.M. also had continual disagreements with the drama critics of *America*, *Catholic World* and *Commonweal* over play evaluations.

The organization disbanded in 1939, but revived for a brief period in 1940.

The Catholic Dramatic Movement

The Catholic Dramatic Movement (not to be confused with the Catholic Theatre Movement) was founded by Father Mathias Helfen in Milwaukee in 1923. Father Helfen, concerned about the lack of suitable plays for his parish drama group, had decided to write his own play. Several other plays followed and Helfen arranged to have them printed and made available to other parish drama groups. This resulted in the Catholic Dramatic Movement which subsequently included an information bureau, a costume rental department, training workshops and publications on practical theatre. Although Helfen envisioned it as national in scope, the movement never gained much of a following outside parish and school drama groups in the Midwest. The basic objective of the group was to counter-balance the "moral excesses" of the contemporary stage through a positive approach of presenting well-produced moral plays. The group, however, depended heavily on religious plays, often of poor quality, and de-emphasized nonreligious ones. Though the group lasted almost thirty years, it was "an essay in persistence rather than a chapter in dramatic arts," said Leo Brady.[41]

It is important to note, however, that one of Father Helfen's desires had always been the creation of a professional Catholic theatre. He wrote in 1937, "We cannot hope to convert Broadway, nor Hollywood, but we can create a professional Catholic theatre."[42]

Dramatic Criticism in Catholic Publications

Father John Talbot Smith, editor of the New York-based *Catholic Review*, introduced the first theatre column into an American Catholic publication in 1889. The column included interviews with Catholic actors and producers and, in spite of canonical prohibitions, reviews by Father Smith of current plays. Despite the reservations of Archbishop Michael Corrigan, Smith continued to write the column until he resigned the editorship in 1891.[43]

Not until 1922 did another Catholic publication begin a regular theatre column. In that year the Jesuit weekly, *America*, hired Elizabeth Jordan to write a periodic column about the New York theatre. The *Catholic World*, a distinguished magazine founded by the Paulist Fathers in 1865, added Euphemia van Rensselaer Wyatt to its staff in January 1923. And in November 1924 the first issue of *Commonweal*, a Catholic magazine published by lay men and women, appeared. Richard Dana Skinner made his debut as *Commonweal*'s drama critic in that issue.[44]

Just because all three were Catholic publications did not mean that they agreed in their play reviews. Michael F. Kelly states that "the conservative *America* tended to emphasize moral aspects of the drama, the liberal *Commonweal* considered its dramatic merits, while the moderate *Catholic World* ranged between the two."[45] The divergence of their views can be seen in their individual treatment of Sidney Howard's *They Knew What They Wanted*. Miss Jordan said, "The play has a sordid theme."[46] Mrs. Wyatt wrote: "Most of the play is none too agreeable . . . there are certain expressions which consensus of opinion has barred from the stage since the days of the

Restoration dramatists."[47] However, Mr. Skinner called the play "a strong and at times powerful lesson in what true Christian love and forgiveness can accomplish in face of almost inevitable disaster."[48]

Just as the critics for the three major Catholic magazines did not always agree with one another, they were also occasionally at odds with the bulletin published by the Catholic Theatre Movement. When the C.T.M. Bulletin issued a harsh condemnation of Elmer Rice's *Street Scene*, Mrs. Wyatt, siding with her two colleagues, said of the play,

> Out of the pitiful tragedy that engulfs her mother and father Rose emerges, bravely struggling. In the fire of that cruel moment, she sees the flicker of a great truth. . . each soul must be a citadel to itself. No enemy can wreck that citadel unless we first open the gates. . . In other words, the kingdom of God lies within us.[49]

Michael Kelley praises Jordan, Skinner and Wyatt for their efforts in bringing dramatic criticism of a respectable quality to the American Catholic press.

Even though the moral consideration remained an important factor, the attempt was made to frame all judgment in artistic terms and the purely moral judgment was abjured. Furthermore, the part was not cause for condemning the whole. Though the part might be criticized by the reviewer, credit was still given where credit was due. Nor was the harmless comedy given blanket praise for its cleanliness, if it lacked dramatic quality. The Catholic press was at last realizing its responsibility in its criticism of the theatre.[50]

The National Catholic Theatre Conference

In 1936 in an article in *America*, playwright Emmet Lavery called for the creation of a national Catholic theatre organization. Lavery advanced the idea on two grounds.

> 1. It is sound economics. Most parishes have the equipment. Most parishes have their share of ambitious young collegians to handle such an assignment. We have the equipment, the personnel, the audience. And . . . the material is infinite and varied.
> 2. It is good Catholic culture. It is an art form particularly Catholic in its development, and it is one medium readily available through which the masses of our people may be made to feel the spark which we call the Catholic way of life.[51]

Lavery pointed out that there were, at the time, over 15,000 Catholic parishes in the United States. If in the following five years, only five percent devoted themselves to establishing a parish theatre, Lavery continued, "who can say that a new Abbey might not rise in America?"[52] Lavery sought to bring about an integration of Catholic ideals of art and morality with American theatrical culture.

The first to respond to Lavery's call was Charles Costello, director of the Loyola Community Theatre in Chicago, who offered to host a meeting of Catholics involved in the theatre. Four hundred and sixteen delegates from twenty-eight states attended the meeting held in Chicago in June, 1937.[53] In August the group met jointly with the Blackfriars' Summer Institute of Dramatic Art at the Catholic University of America in Washington, D.C. They officially inaugurated the new organization there and named it "The National Catholic Theatre Conference." They chose Dr. John H. Mahoney as their first president and established a permanent office at Catholic University.

In 1938 the organization had 235 individual members and 128 organizational members.[54] The N.C.T.C. defined as its purpose "the dissemination of Catholic theatre in harmony with Catholic spirit and philosophy," but its early years were marked by disputes over the precise relation of "Catholic" and "theatre."[55] By means of a monthly bulletin, an annual survey and periodic conventions, the organization strove by an exchange of information to propose ideals and elevate the standard of production. In 1941 the headquarters moved to the Blackfriars Theatre in New York. The organization continued for over thirty years. At its height in 1964, it had over 14,000 members, mainly from school and parish groups.

The Founding of the National Blackfriars Guild

Father Urban Nagle, O.P., was born Edward Nagle in Providence, Rhode Island in 1905. His father was a theatre fireman at the Providence Opera House and from an early age Nagle saw all the shows which played Providence for free, including *The Emperor Jones* with Charles Gilpin.[56] He credited those "Annie Oakleys" (complimentary tickets) with sparking his love of the theatre. At the age of eighteen he entered the Dominican Order and received the name Urban. He studied at the Order's institutions in Rhode Island, Ohio and Washington, D.C.

In 1929, while a student brother studying for the priesthood at the Dominican House of Studies on the campus of the Catholic University of America in Washington, Nagle entered a playwrighting contest sponsored by the Longman Green Publishing Company. He wrote a passion play called *Barter* and it won first prize. Later, in 1930, the pastor of Saint Dominic's Church in Washington asked the prior (superior) of the Dominican House of Studies if Brother Urban could produce *Barter* as a Lenten production for his parish. The prior consented and Brother Urban asked a seminary classmate, Brother Fabian Carey, to take charge of the sets.

Carey, born Thomas Carey in Chicago in 1904, was orphaned at the age of twelve. The local parish priest was given custody of young Tom and arranged for him to be educated at Campion Academy, a prestigious Jesuit preparatory school in Wisconsin. He worked as a draftsman in Chicago for a year and then entered the Dominican Order where he received the name Fabian.[57]

Carey's and Nagle's production of *Barter* at Saint Dominic's enjoyed great success and the venture gave the two students the inspiration for the Blackfriars Guild which they founded in 1931. At first they envisioned it as a local Catholic theatre group for Washington. (Their first production was Philip Barry's *Holiday*).[58] Later, however, Nagle envisioned a series of Catholic theatre groups (Blackfriars Guilds) across the country.

After ordination in 1931 their superiors assigned both Carey and Nagle to pursue, for reasons known only to the Church, doctorates in psychology at the Catholic University of America. They continued to work with the Washington Blackfriars Guild and to oversee the new chapters in other cities. There were eventually twenty-two Blackfriars chapters: in Rochester, Minneapolis-Saint Paul, Philadelphia, Springfield (Illinois), Cleveland, Albany, Brooklyn, Boston, New Orleans, Troy (New York), Chicago, Pittsburgh, Providence, Dayton, Madison, Louisville, San Antonio, Lowell (Massachusetts), New Haven, Grand Rapids, Washington, D.C. and later New York City. Blackfriars even operated a summer theatre at Nabnasset, Massachusetts.[59]

The stated purpose of all the Blackfriars Guilds was to devote themselves "to producing plays of artistic merit which reflect the

spiritual nature of man and his eternal destiny."[60] In 1936 in an article
in *Sign* magazine, Father Nagle elaborated on this stated purpose.

> We have had parish dramatics for many years. But really, what have
> they done for the drama as such? As a matter of fact, they have not been
> designed to help the drama. Rather the parishes have called upon the
> drama to help them -- to raise money for worthy projects, to bring about
> social enjoyment and intercourse, and to provide a certain amount of
> entertainment for the local parishioners. The Blackfriars Guild, however,
> has no interest in this parochial viewpoint. Its field is national, its
> dramatic scope universal, its proximate ideal sublimely conceived. We
> must make ourselves absolutely independent of Broadway. We must not
> go to Broadway even for our plays, for we are to form within ourselves
> a staff of writers who will furnish us with material for our productions.
> In that way, we need not compromise our ideals. We know what we
> want and we will create it.[61]

Later in the same article, Nagle spoke of the need for the Church
and the theatre to work together and set forth his ideas about the
amateur status of Blackfriars.

> Today there is no reason why the church and the theatre should fight
> against each other. The dramatic instinct in all of us is too strong to be
> suppressed. Cannot the theatre be used as a medium to bring beauty and
> high idealism into the lives of everyone? Can it not play a constructive
> part in the building of great characters upon which the future of the
> world depends? It can, indeed. But this sublimination of the theatre can
> be accomplished only by amateurs. The professional stage is too
> dependent on box office receipts. Accordingly, it is of amateurs that our
> Guild is composed, men and women who understand the great and
> inherent power of a National Catholic Theatre, and are willing to
> sacrifice personal comfort and remuneration to the attainment of an
> ideal.[62]

After finishing his degree in 1934 Father Nagle was assigned to
teach at Providence College in Providence, Rhode Island, where, of
course, he founded a chapter of the Blackfriars Guild. Father Carey
was assigned to teach at the Catholic University of America and
continued to direct the Washington chapter. In 1937 Nagle and Carey
set up the Blackfriars Institute of Dramatic Art, a summer program for
training actors, directors and designers, at Catholic University. In

1940 this summer institute separated from Blackfriars and became the drama department of Catholic University which Father Gilbert V. Hartke, O.P., headed for more than thirty years.

In 1940 Father Nagle's superiors transferred him to Saint Vincent Ferrer Priory at Sixty-fifth Street and Lexington Avenue in New York to edit the *Holy Name Journal*, the official publication of the Holy Name Society. Nagle requested his superiors to assign Father Carey to New York also, ostensibly to help with the *Holy Name Journal*. However, editing the *Holy Name Journal* was not a demanding job. And since they now found themselves located in Manhattan Nagle and Carey had the opportunity to pursue their interest in Catholic theatre in New York.

The New York Theatre at the Time Blackfriars Began

Founded in 1940, the New York Blackfriars Theatre had its first production in the fall of 1941. The New York theatre at the time was in a state of transition. It had just come out of the creative decade of the 1930's and was beginning to feel the approach of war.

Although the nation had undergone its worst economic depression in the 1930's, the theatre had never been stronger. John Mason Brown referred to the thirties as "those full lean years."[63] It had been a decade dominated by playwrights. Eugene O'Neill won the Nobel Prize for Literature in that decade and produced *Mourning Becomes Electra, Ah, Wilderness* and *Days Without End*. Robert Sherwood wrote *Reunion in Vienna, The Petrified Forest, Abe Lincoln in Illinois* and *Idiot's Delight*. Sidney Howard penned *The Late Christopher Bean, Dodsworth* and *Yellow Jack*. Maxwell Anderson turned out ten plays during the decade, the best of which were *High Tor* and *Winterset*. Among Clifford Odets' successful plays in the thirties were *Waiting for Lefty, Awake and Sing* and *The Golden Boy*. Lillian Hellman came onto the scene with *The Children's Hour* and *The Little Foxes*. Promising new playwrights Thornton Wilder and William Saroyan arrived on Broadway in the late 1930's. S. N. Behrman, Philip Barry and the team of George S. Kaufman and Moss Hart were writing comedy. George Gershwin, Jerome Kern, Cole Porter and Rodgers and Hart brought new vitality and maturity to the American musical.

The Broadway season 1940-1941, the year Blackfriars opened, was a particularly fine one. Ethel Barrymore starred in Emlyn Williams' *The Corn is Green*. Robert Sherwood won the Pulitzer Prize for *There Shall Be No Night* which starred Alfred Lunt and Lynn Fontaine. *Johnny Belinda* and *My Sister Eileen* played to full houses while the big musical that year was *Cabin in the Sky* with Ethel Waters. In addition, several impressive revivals brightened the season: Jose Ferrer in *Charley's Aunt*, Laurence Olivier and Vivien Leigh in *Romeo and Juliet*, Helen Hayes and Maurice Evans in *Twelfth Night*, Ingrid Bergman and Burgess Meredith in *Liliom*, and Sara Algood and Barry Fitzgerald in *Juno and the Paycock*.[64]

The calibre of dramatic writing and production in the Broadway theatre was probably higher than at any other time in its history. It would prove a difficult task for Blackfriars to compete with the Broadway theatre, especially in the acquisition of scripts.

Along with the creative surge in playwrighting came new boldness and frankness. Playwrights treated topics never before mentioned in the theatre. *The Green Bay Tree*, for example, dealt with the topic of homosexuality, and *Tobacco Road* included a scene in which Jeeter Lester and his daughter gape into the open window of their shack while Jeeter's son and his bride consummate their marriage inside. Such plays shocked and offended many people, including numerous Catholics. In reviewing Broadway offerings during one season, *America* magazine referred to them as "theatrical sewers."[65] Even *Billboard* in 1933 lamented the portrayal of women in current plays: "It is seldom now that we see a lady depicted behind the footlights. Harridans, prostitutes and wenches make up the female population of our plays."[66] There were clearly some people looking for a tamer and gentler theatre.

The depression of the 1930's had also brought with it greater social activism in the theatre. In 1929 John Howard Lawson had started the New Playwrights Theatre which presented plays that sought to advance the cause of the working class. That same year twelve ethnic theatre groups formed the Workers' Dramatic Council and began publishing *Workers' Theatre*. In 1932 the First National Workers' Theatre Festival and Conference was held in New York. Delegates formed the National League of Workers' Theatres and affiliated with the International Workers' Dramatic Union.[67] Other theatre groups, not necessarily "workers' theatres," became concerned with issues of social justice. The Yiddish Art Theatre staged a pro-Soviet play, *Armoured Train No. 1469* and the Group Theatre produced *1931*, a drama of the unemployment crisis.[68] Many people were concerned about the socialist leanings of some theatre artists and others suspected Communist infiltration in the theatre. In 1931 in an article entitled, "The Theatre as a Weapon," *America* decried the plethora of pro-communist propaganda plays. The primary principle, the magazine said, seemed to be that such plays must be "entirely agitative, anti-capitalist, anti-religious, anti-bourgeouis propaganda . . . the themes must always be clearly, loudly communistic."[69] The article went on to call for the production of plays to counter this theatrical "threat." It is clear, then, that there existed at least a small audience for a patriotic, pro-religious and anti-communist theatre.

Besides the Broadway and workers' theatres, there was other theatrical activity in New York. Ethnic theatre groups were quite active. Unfortunately Eva LaGallienne's Civic Repertory had closed in 1931. However, though no one used the term "Off-Broadway" yet, small experimental groups did produce plays at such places as the Provincetown Playhouse, Heckscher Little Theatre, the Little Theatre, the Roof of the Hotel Sutton and the Craig Theatre.[70] Most of these had fleeting existences. New York in 1940 was ready for a more stable experimental theatre where new scripts could be tried out and where young actors could gain experience and be seen by audiences and agents. Blackfriars hoped to fill this gap and advance the cause of "Catholic theatre" in the bargain.

1. By professional level I mean a theatre in which the actors make their living primarily by acting. Although Blackfriars paid salaries to its actors for only one year (1956-7) it depended on people who were primarily theatre or television actors looking for a showcase for their talents, rather than on amateurs.

2. Program for *Shepherds on the Shelf* by Rev. John P. O'Connell, Oct. 11-Nov. 19, 1960. Blackfriars Collection, archives of the Providence College Library, Providence, R. I.

3. Howard Greenberger, *The Off-Broadway Experience* (Englewood Cliffs, N.J.: Prentice-Hall, Inc., 1971), 14.

4. Stuart W. Little, *Off-Broadway: The Prophetic Theatre* (New York: Coward, McCann and Geoghegan, Inc., 1972), 14.

5. Julia S. Price, *The Off-Broadway Theatre* (New York: Scarecrow Press, 1962).

6. Robert Louis Hobbs, "Off-Broadway: The Early Years" (Ph.D. diss., Northwestern University 1964).

7. This explains why Dominicans place the initials "O.P." behind their names: Order of Preachers.

8. The Dominican Order is actually a family of orders, consisting of separate and independent orders of friars, cloistered nuns, sisters and affiliated lay men and women.

9. William A. Hinnebusch, O.P., *The History of the Dominican Order*, Vol. I (Staten Island, N.Y.: Alba House, 1966), 94.

10. Sister Mary Jean Dorcy, O.P., *Saint Dominic's Family* (Dubuque: Priory Press, 1963), 115.

11. All of the information on the Blackfriars priory and theatre is from: Irwin Smith, *Shakespeare's Blackfriars Playhouse* (New York: New York University Press, 1964).

12. William A. Hinnebusch, O.P., *The Dominicans: A Short History* (Staten Island, N.Y.: Alba House, 1975), 119.

13. John Cogley, *Catholic America* (Garden City, N.Y.: Image Books, 1974), 1 and 46.

14. Cogley, 116.

15. Cogley, 8.

16. Cogley, 136.

17. Cogley, 136.

18. Cogley, 117.

19. Cogley, 135.

20. Cogley, 138.

21. Archbishop John Carroll et al, "Pastoral Letter to the Clergy," 10 November, 1810 in Peter Guilday, *A History of the Councils of Baltimore: 1791-1884* (New York: Arno Press & The New York Times, 1969), 74.

22. *Concilii Plenarii Baltimorensis II; Acta et Decreta* (Baltimore: Joannes

Murphy, 1868), 95.

23. Father James Hinnen, interview by author, telephone, 19 October 1981.

24. Frances Panchok, "The Catholic Church and the Theatre in New York, 1890 - 1920," (Ph.D. diss., Catholic University of America 1976), 36-37.

25. *Concilii Plenarii Baltimorensis III: Acta et Decreta* (Baltimore: Joannes Murphy, 1866), 42. English translation: A well-known axiom among the Fathers of the Church held that many things which are allowable for lay persons are not fitting for clerics. Therefore, in order to preserve the honor and decency of ecclesiastical orders, we command that priests abstain from attendance at public horse races, public theatres and public spectacles.

26. "Questions and Answers," *Homiletic and Pastoral Review*, 36 (August, 1936), 1188-9. Underlining is mine. All further quotations in the paragraph following are from this article.

27. Panchok, 45.

28. Panchok, 498.

29. "The Stage," *America*, 10 May 1913, 112-113.

30. Panchock, 501.

31. "Farley Recognizes Catholic Players," *New York Times*, 2 February 1915.

32. *Catholic News*, 4 June 1921. 6.

33. *Catholic News*, 29 April 1922. 4.

34. *Catholic News*, 25 October 1919. 4.

35. *Catholic News*, 15 June 1912. 2.

36. Michael Francis Kelly, "The Reaction of the Catholic Church to the Commercial Theatre in New York City, 1900 to 1958," Diss. State University of Iowa 1959, 52.

37. *Catholic News*, 11 October 1913. 3.

38. Kelly, 60.

39. Kelly, 62.

40. Kelly, 222.

41. Leo Brady, "Catholic Theatre Movement," *New Catholic Encyclopedia* (1966).

42. Kelly, 106-107.

43. Panchok, 454-457.

44. It is interesting to note that although both *America* and *Catholic World* were (and are) published by religious orders, both hired lay people as drama critics. It appears that there was still a stigma to a priest seeing and reviewing plays.

45. Kelly, 163.

46. Elizabeth Jordan, "The Stage," *America*, 31 January 1925. 377.

47. Euphemia Van Rensselaer Wyatt, "The Drama," *Catholic World*, 120 (January 1925), 523.

48. R. Dana Skinner, "The Play," *Commonweal*, 24 December 1924. 189.

49. Euphemia Van Rensselaer Wyatt, "The Drama," *Catholic World*, 128 (March 1929), 721-722.

50. Kelly, 142-143.

51. Emmet Lavery, "The Catholic Theatre: New Thought on Old Form," *America*, 5 December 1936, 197.

52. Lavery, 198.

53. Sister Mary Michael Keefe, "The National Catholic Theatre Conference: Its Aims and Achievements," Diss. Northwestern Unviersity 1965, 31.

54. Brady.

55. Brady.

56. Urban Nagle, O.P., *Behind the Masque* (New York: McMullen Books, Inc., 1951), 3.

57. James Reginald Coffey, O.P., *Pictorial History of the Dominican Province of Saint Joseph* (New York: Holy Name Society, 1946), 325.

58. Nagle, 25.

59. Most Blackfriars chapters had short and undistinguished existences. After the founding of the New York theatre, Nagle and Carey devoted less and less attention to the other chapters. Some ceased operation and others affiliated with the National Catholic Theatre Conference. In the 1960's only one other Blackfriars Guild remained, a completely separate and independent chapter in Dayton, Ohio.

60. "The Blackfriars: Experiment in Good Theatre," *Catholic Preview of Entertainment*, 1 (December 1956), 57.

61. Mary Fabyan Windeatt, "Blackfriars Guild," *Sign*, 16 (December 1936), 285.

62. Windeatt, 285.

63. Brooks Atkinson, *Broadway* (New York: Macmillan Publishing Co., 1974), 291.

64. The information in this paragraph is from Daniel Blum, *A Pictorial History of the American Theatre, 1960 - 1976*, 4th ed. (New York: Crown Publishers, 1977), 188-290.

65. "Our Theatrical Sewers," *America*, 23 August 1930, 477.

66. Editorial, *Billboard*, 7 January 1933, 24.

67. Oscar G. Brockett and Robert R. Findlay, *Century of Innovation* (Englewood Cliffs, N.J.: Prentice-Hall, Inc., 1973), pp. 507-508.

68. Richard F. Grady, S.J., "The Theatre as a Weapon," *America*, 16 January 1932, 364.

69. Grady, 365.

70. Julia S. Price, *The Off-Broadway Theatre* (New York: The Scarecrow Press, 1962), 18-19.

CHAPTER 2
THE BEGINNING: 1940-1945

Before the establishment of Blackfriars Eliza O'Brien Loomis had proposed the Excelsior Theatre and both Father John Talbot Smith and Father Mathias Helfen conceived of a professional Catholic playhouse. None of these proposals moved out of the idea stage.

Father Nagle felt strongly about the lack of a Catholic theatre for New York.

> It might be a source of humiliation -- if anybody bothered to think about it -- that while we have a Yiddish theatre, an Irish theatre, a Federal Theatre Project, a flock of communistic theatres, we have not achieved, at least with a national recognition, a Catholic theatre. It might further provoke some thought to mull over the fact that in every other art form and propaganda medium (if you will) the Catholics have done something about it.[1]

Now he and Father Carey found themselves in New York with almost ten years of their local Catholic theatre venture behind them. They had almost two dozen Blackfriars chapters to draw upon for support, and they felt that an audience existed for a religious and more family-oriented drama than most Broadway theatres offered. They reasoned that Catholics who had supported Catholic newspapers, magazines and radio programs might also support a Catholic theatre. Also, in this day before Off-Broadway, there would be very little competition from other non-Broadway theatres. This meant that a Catholic theatre would be able to depend on countless young actors

4 CHAPTER 2

and technicians eager to gain experience. Lastly, Nagle thought that a Catholic theatre provided a positive approach to remedying the things that he and some other Catholics felt were wrong with the theatre. He wrote: "If negative censorship is sufficient ... why not throw out Catholic schools and resort to telling the public schools through legislation what they may not teach? Consistency!"[2] So, despite the harbingers of war, the two priests decided that the time had come for a Catholic theatre for New York.

In the fall of 1940 they sent out a letter to a few hundred cause-minded Catholics in the New York area, asking for donations. The response disappointed them but they decided to forge ahead anyway. In November someone told them about a former Y.M.C.A. auditorium on the second floor of a building on West Fifty-seventh Street that was empty and available for rent. Father Nagle reported.

> It had no proscenium, no switchboard, in fact, not much of anything except uncomfortable seats in various degrees of repair and a most inadequate stage in front of an old fashioned concert shell. Perhaps the feature which dated it most accurately was a dimmer board for gas lights.[3]

Because of the poor state of the auditorium the rent was inexpensive and the two friars decided to rent it. Father Carey then spent the following spring and summer renovating the little theatre. He and a few friends built a proscenium arch and bought, borrowed or asked for equipment as donations. They purchased the front curtain, for example, for fifty dollars from Gypsy Rose Lee's show at the World's Fair.[4]

The theatre, which had both an orchestra and balcony, seated 383 people.[5] The stage was small -- twenty-four feet wide and sixteen feet deep.[6] There were men's and women's dressing rooms one flight up from the stage and several large rooms in the back of the auditorium which could be used for costume and property storage, scene shop and offices. A lobby and box office were on the ground floor.[7]

Nagle and Carey made the decision to produce original plays. This had long been an ideal of Nagle's. He did not wish the New York Blackfriars to be like other little theatres in the country. "If we follow the majority of little theatres throughout the country and clamor for cast-off Broadway successes -- perhaps preferring the most innocuous to prove our good negative Catholicity, we might as well not bother having been born."[8] Nagle felt strongly that the fostering of new plays which "reflect the spiritual nature of man and his eternal destiny" and "which solve their fundamental problems in the light of Catholic philosophy" should be one of the primary tasks of Blackfriars.

> If the drama is one of the most potent means of conveying ideas and ideals, it is highly essential that the Church employ the drama to instruct and inspire, and the first and most important step . . . must be the writing of drama through which Catholic truth shall shine to the world in undiminished splendor. This is in fact the very essence of the Catholic theatre movement. The actual operation of theatres and the presentation of plays is relatively unimportant. If the Church can produce dramas worth presenting, they will be enacted whether we have theatres or not. On the other hand, a Catholic theatre without Catholic drama of approved merit is doomed to death in its birth. Only things which are true can live forever.[9]

Father Nagle envisioned Blackfriars as "a clearing house for plays which will concern itself with high artistry rather than profit. Artistry in a sound philosophical sense has much to do with truth and beauty."[10]

The other Blackfriars chapters had been unable to produce original plays. Nagle felt that there existed no better place than New York to attempt to do it. He had an additional reason for doing new plays.

> We thought there was little point in doing a play which had been done better down the street ten years ago or in Greece 2,500 years ago. Life was moving on and new plays were either reflecting patterns or determining norms. That was our business if we could justify this theatrical side-line at all.[11]

Nagle contacted the Dramatists' Guild of New York and they proved to be cooperative. They sent out word to their members that the Blackfriars Guild was looking for plays. They told playwrights to send or bring their scripts to an address which was also the editorial office of the *Holy Name Journal*. The response was overwhelming and the scripts poured in. The notice from the Dramatists' Guild, however, had not mentioned the religious character of Blackfriars. Many of the playwrights were surprised to arrive at the address, with script in hand, and to find a priest dressed in a white habit. Nagle described their reaction.

> Some laughed aloud at the door, some apologized (for what wasn't clear), some became suddenly pious, some employed a little high pressure, some fled. One stately woman in a huge picture hat stopped cold at the door, stared at me in a sort of terror and blurted, "Oh! Oh! You won't want my plays. They're much too dirty."[12]

Out of the hundreds of plays submitted some were good. A few of them were exceptionally good, but they had production demands that at the time the little theatre couldn't meet. Those plays worth considering and not out of reach because of physical requirements, "had the taint of Broadway."[13] Some authors offered to "tone-down" their plays for a Catholic audience. Nagle reacted.

> It was so difficult to explain that we weren't concerned with how close to a line we might walk, but rather that we wanted a theatre with a spiritual lift. We weren't merely trying to get by the Watch and Ward Society or plotting to escape being closed by the police. We were starting from the other end and wanted to give people a good theatre -- good in the sense that Aristotle and Thomas Aquinas meant when they talked about art.[14]

Finally Nagle read a play written by a fellow Dominican, Father Brendan Larnen, O.P. Father Larnen, an Irish-born priest assigned to New York, had previously written a play for the Washington Blackfriars entitled *Nothing Begins*. His new play, *Up the Rebels*, was a comedy-drama about the Irish Rebellion. Larnen said he decided to write the play because 1941 was the twenty-fifth anniversary of the Easter Rising of 1916 and also because pressure was then being put on Ireland to enter the war on the side of the British. Larnen stated that he wanted to show that Ireland had little reason to come to Britain's defense.[15] The result was *Up the Rebels*, which Larnen wrote under the pen name, Sean Vincent.

Now that they had a play, the friars decided to aim for a fall production. Nagle and Carey interviewed at least a dozen directors. All were enthusiastic until they found out that Blackfriars wasn't sure if it could pay a salary. Through mutual acquaintances they contacted Dennis Gurney, an Englishman who would direct the majority of

Blackfriars plays for eighteen years.

Gurney had been born in England, the son of theatrical parents -- Gurney's father, Edmund, played the original Mr. Doolittle in *Pygmalion* in both London and New York. Young Gurney had worked at a variety of jobs before going into the theatre himself, including farming in western Canada. His first professional role in the theatre was in 1922 in *Aren't We All?* with Cyril Maude and Leslie Howard. He subsequently appeared in over twenty Broadway productions, "mostly flops," he said.[16] He ran his own stock company in Stamford, Connecticut which included Robert Montgomery. Gurney was out of work and recuperating from a broken toe when he heard from a friend that Blackfriars needed a director. The priests told Gurney that they couldn't offer him any salary at the time and added that they weren't sure when they could pay him. Gurney responded, "I'd rather do something I like than discuss salary."[17] Gurney feared that his not being a Catholic would be a problem, but Nagle and Carey assured him it was not. Gurney would remain with Blackfriars until 1959. Actress Geraldine Page recalled how Gurney shattered her stereotype of Blackfriars. She remembered him "screaming about his beer and cussing and carrying on. He seemed incongruous in the setting. Being Protestant I thought things should be reverent and proper at all times."[18]

Now that Blackfriars had a play, a theatre and a director, Nagle thought it was time to secure whatever legal permits he needed for the New York Blackfriars. He later wrote,

> It seems that in opening a theatre in this city [New York] the problems of actors and scripts and location are utterly incidental. One must get permission from what are called "departments." A subdivision of the problem is to find out the names and addresses of these departments from which one must get permission.[19]

Being the son of a fireman, Nagle started with the New York Fire Department. The Fire Department informed him that he was under the jurisdiction of the Division of Public Assemblies. Chief O'Donohue of the Division of Public Assemblies told Nagle that before his department could act "you must get a certificate of occupancy from the Department of Housing and Building, and if you make any changes you must apply to the Departments of Standards and

Appeals, and I'm sure you've seen the Commissioner of Licenses."[20] The Department of Licenses, however, told Nagle that, as a charitable and educational organization, Blackfriars did not need a license as long as it posted in the box office an affidavit setting forth its non-profit status. The Housing and Building Department stated that since Nagle wanted to operate a theatre and not a drama school he was out of their jurisdiction, but should proceed to the Department of Standards and Appeals. Standards and Appeals informed him that the building was classified as a Y.M.C.A. and if Blackfriars made any changes they would have to bring in twelve sets of blueprints and Standards and Appeals would pass them on to a higher department.

The perplexed and frustrated priest went back to Chief O'Donohue of Public Assemblies to see if he could, perhaps, cut through the bureaucracy. O'Donohue had in the meantime sent an inspector over to Blackfriars and had a two page list of items that the theatre needed to be brought up to code. However, when O'Donohue found out that Blackfriars didn't need to be licensed, he sent Nagle directly to the Department of Fire Prevention. The Department of Fire Prevention settled for a few fire extinguishers. With that Nagle assumed that Blackfriars met all of the various codes for the City of New York.

Despite Nagle's praise of the purity of amateur theatre and the inability to pay actors, he intended to get the best actors possible. The priests approached Actors Equity Association for approval to use Equity actors who were between jobs and who would be willing to work without pay. "Equity graciously and promptly agreed, knowing that its members primarily wanted to act," said Nagle. "We were chartered as an educational and charitable institution and were so obviously not exploiting people's labor for profit that Equity welcomed the new experiment."[21] They had, however, an unwritten understanding with Equity that if an actor found a salaried job during the rehearsal or run of a Blackfriars play that he or she would be free to leave the production.

Blackfriars finally managed to open its first production, *Up the Rebels*, for a three performance run on Oct. 30, 1941. Orchestra seats cost $1.10 and balcony seats $.83. Gurney directed and Edward Rutyna, who had worked with the Lowell, Massachusetts Blackfriars, designed the set. The cast included Liam Dunn, who had previously been in *Waiting for Lefty* and *Dead End*.[22] The play, set in contemporary Ireland with a flashback to the years 1916-1920, told the story of two young men, playmates in their youth, who were on opposite sides in the struggle for Irish independence. In the course of time, however, the one in the British uniform joins the rebels, and the rebel becomes a Free Stater. In the end both are killed. Louis Calta, who reviewed the production for the *New York Times* called the play "an earnest drama of violent emotions and conflicting ideas," and said it was played by a "competent cast."[23] Bide Dudley of WHN-Radio said, "I went to see it expecting to find an amateurish effort. Instead I found a well-written play, well-acted and directed -- one with enough substance to make anyone think."[24] The play was so well received that it was scheduled for a fourth performance. The New York Blackfriars was now in operation.

For its second production, Nagle chose *Song Out of Sorrow*, a play by Boston attorney Felix Doherty about the life of Francis Thompson. Thompson (1859-1907) was an English poet whose most famous works were "Ode to the Setting Sun" and "The Hound of Heaven." Many of his works dealt with religious themes and were especially popular with Catholics. The Boston Blackfriars had previously presented the play with British actor Robert Speaight playing Thompson. Father Nagle thought the play should be given a New York production.

The play related how Thompson's platonic friendship with a Cockney prostitute, Flossie, helped him to overcome his drug addiction and to begin writing his best works. In the end Flossie sacrificed her relationship with Thompson. Stacy Harris, who had played Jack Armstrong on the radio series, "Jack Armstrong--All American Boy," played Thompson; Rosanna Seaborn was Flossie; and Guy Spaull, who had been the first tempter in the original production of *Murder in the Cathedral*, played Bill, Flossie's common-law husband.

Ben Bradford of the *New York Times* said of the production,

> The torture endured in the mind of the poet during these days and his final creation of great poetry was extremely well presented by the author. At no time did he let the tragic overtones of the play become maudlin or superficial. He knew his subject well and made it come to life.[25]

Bradford went on to say that Stacy Harris had given a sensitive characterization as Thompson and praised the cast as a whole. Robert

Francis of the *Brooklyn Eagle* wrote that *Song Out of Sorrow* was "a tender and touching play . . . one of the season's most rewarding."[26]

Though only Blackfriars' second production, *Song Out of Sorrow* was one of its most acclaimed and, certainly, one of the best-written. Father Nagle recalled one anecdote from the production. A well-known producer said to him after the final curtain, "I don't get it. You have prostitutes and dope fiends and it's a Catholic theatre. I have them and it's cops."[27] Unfortunately *Song Out of Sorrow* opened four days after the bombing of Pearl Harbor and few people came to the performances. Blackfriars revived the play in 1955.

In January 1942 the United States Trust Company, who had recently purchased the building, ordered an inspection made of the theatre and sent Blackfriars a letter that it would have to close down. Father Carey dealt with the new owners who referred him to the Department of Housing and Building. Housing and Building informed Carey that the theatre violated a particular section of the Administrative Code of the City of New York and suggested he file an application for variation with the Board of Standards and Appeals. After lengthy discussions at Standards and Appeals, an official there finally suggested that Blackfriars remove eighty-four seats from the theatre. Having only 299 seats would put the theatre in a different category and jurisdiction. So Father Carey returned to the theatre and removed eighty-four seats. Stuart W. Little wrote in *Off-Broadway: The Prophetic Theatre* that in 1947 Morton Gottlieb had all but 299 seats ripped out of the New Stages playhouse in order to circumvent city fire and building regulations.[28] He states that "ever since the number 299 has defined the allowable maximum size of a theatre" for Off-Broadway. This was five years after Father Carey did the same thing at Blackfriars.

For its third production in February the group produced an innocuous family farce, *The Years Between*, which Father Nagle wrote under the pen name, Richard Burbage. Brooks Atkinson gave a tepid review.[29]

Atkinson's review had more effect than he knew. The following day Nagle received a letter from License Commissioner Moss: "I noticed in today's paper an article by Brooks Atkinson in which he indicates that there is a regular performance going on in your theatre. Please call here on Monday."[30] At the meeting, Moss stated that if Blackfriars was getting reviews from practically all of the papers, it was a "regular theatre" and should be licensed. Father Nagle objected to this because a license for a theatre with three hundred seats cost a hundred dollars. After lengthy correspondence and several interviews, Blackfriars reluctantly purchased a license.

For its last show of the season the theatre group decided to do another play written by Nagle, *Savonarola*. This time Nagle did not use a pen name. The play offered the group two challenges. It required a large, all-male cast and the leading character had been the center of a 450-year controversy. Girolamo Savonarola (1452-1498), Florentine Dominican friar, was both a political and religious reformer. His rigid views brought him into conflict with the artists and politicians of the period and ultimately with Pope Alexander VI. After confessing, under torture, to heresy and schism, he was burned at the stake. As early as 1499, however, many venerated him as a saint. The sixteenth century Dominican saint, Catherine Di Ricci, in fact, prayed to him. The play centered on the conflict of individual conscience and authority. Unfortunately, Nagle set the play in the common room of the Dominican priory of San Marco and had the characters talk about the important events that were happening elsewhere in the city.

The reviews of the production were mixed. Robert Coleman of the *Daily Mirror* said *Savonarola*

> is a stimulating and moving play. Father Nagle has given us a thoughtful, vivid picture of a valiant man and an exciting era and he has enriched it with a philosophy and understanding that is timely and timeless, important and dramatic. Savonarola is the type of drama which most commerical managements would hesitate to produce, but it merits production. The Blackfriars Guild deserves praise for having made its presentation possible.[31]

However, Robert Sylvester wrote in the *Daily News*, "Unfortunately the good padre has in many spots written with an eye to oratory rather than dramatic effect. After a while listening to some of the characters is a little like listening to somebody read an encyclopedia."[32]

Nevertheless, Richard Watts of the *Herald-Tribune* included *Savonarola* in his list of the ten best productions of the 1941-42 season.[33] Blackfriars considered it quite a distinction for an experimental theatre in its first season.

At the end of its first season, 1941-42, Blackfriars had a deficit of

$3,108.01.[34] General expenses for the theatre -- remodeling and equipping the theatre and office, rent, insurance, electricity, telephone, printing and postage -- came to $5,373.72. The rent was $308 a month. Specific expenses involved directly with the production of four plays -- lumber and canvas, properties, costumes, recordings, publicity, and federal amusement tax -- were $1,641.49. That season no salaries at all were paid. Total expenses amounted to $7,015.41. Income from ticket sales was $3,707.40. Additional income for occasional rental of the theatre to outside groups was $200.00, making a total income of $3,907.40. Father Nagle raised the $3,108 necessary to balance the books by appealing to donors.

Though by no means a financial success, Blackfriars had not only survived its first season in New York, but had produced at least two critical successes and had gained the attention of the New York newspapers.

Finances would always remain a problem for the Catholic theatre. Father Nagle recounted one story concerning salaries. Father Brendan Larnen was alone in the office at the theatre one evening when "a statuesque blonde" came in to inquire about Blackfriars productions. Finally she asked Father Larnen how much Blackfriars paid. When he answered that the group didn't pay anything at all, she replied, "Oh, you don't pay anything do you? Why you're the sort of people that keep us girls in burlesque!"[35]

Subsidiary problems in the matter of audiences faced the company at the end of that first year. Father Nagle wrote,

> Did we want to play to the regular theatre clientele or to build new audiences out of the moviegoers? Did we prefer to teach the young something about theatre or to cater to more settled and less noisy audiences? We did talk about these things, but the problem settled itself in a very simple fashion. We tried to produce a variety of scripts and those who liked us came back. Some were young and some were old. Some were veteran theatre-goers and others asked us what time the second show went on. We played to people and asked no questions and made no distinctions -- and that is as it should be.[36]

"The 1942-43 season was one of the worst we've encountered," Nagle recalled.[37] The productions were not generally well received and there was a major conflict with the crafts unions.

The first play of the season, *Inside Story* by Peter Sheehan, was a comedy about a young woman who ran a magazine devoted to various causes from the basement of her parent's home. The cast included J. Augustus Keogh, formerly of Dublin's Abbey Theatre. Joseph Pihodna of the *Herald-Tribune* spoke for most of the reviewers when he wrote that the "Blackfriars Guild . . . is beginning this season on the left foot."[38]

The following production, *Tinker's Dam* by Andrew Hawke, starred vaudeville veteran Jerry Buckley. A fantasy set in a bomb shelter, it had a scientist, a newspaperman, a soldier, his girlfriend and a tinker discuss life and the hereafter. Lewis Nichols of the *Times* wrote that "much of this sort of whimsey seems funnier on script paper than it really is."[39] The cast did include newcomer Eileen Heckart in her first New York appearance.[40] Though not a successful production, it got two good notices for Heckart. Burns Mantle of the *Daily News* said there were "helpful comic touches from Dort Clark and Eileen Heckart,"[41] and Willela Waldorf of the *Post* wrote that "Eileen Heckart is gustily Mae Westian as Mrs. Cow."[42]

A few days after the opening of *Tinker's Dam* Blackfriars had a visit from a representative of Actors Equity Association, with instructions to withdraw members of Equity from the cast because of pressure from the theatre crafts unions. Father Carey went to discuss matters further with union officials and was able to forestall problems with the unions. The problem, however, was not to go away.

The only bright spot in the season was the production of *A Man's House* by John Drinkwater. Drinkwater, an English poet and playwright whose most famous work was *Abraham Lincoln*, had died in 1937. *A Man's House*, one of Drinkwater's lesser known works, had never been given a New York production. The play tells the story of the effect of the crucifixion of Jesus on the members of a wealthy Jerusalem family. Blackfriars was fortunate to be able to cast actor Augustin Duncan as Salathiel, the head of the household. Duncan, the brother of dancer Isadora Duncan, was a veteran of forty-four years in the theatre. He had appeared in many Theatre Guild productions and had played with Paul Robeson, James Cagney, Charles Bickford and Maurice Evans. Duncan had lost his eyesight fourteen years previously but had continued acting. Cavada Humphrey played Salathiel's daughter Esther.[43]

For the production Duncan had to time his entrances to single word cues, to find his way around a stage having several large pieces of

furniture on it, climb stairs, and greet other actors as if he just saw
them enter. Ironically, the play contained a scene in which Duncan
had to lead his "blind" daughter across the stage. Duncan, active in
organizations for the blind, invited fifty young men and women from
the Lighthouse, an institution for the blind, to be his guests for the
opening of the play.[44] Miss Hopkins from the Lighthouse constructed
a model of the set so that the blind guests could touch it before the
performance and get the impression of entrances, exits and furniture
arrangement.

The production was well received by the critics. Shirley Frohlich of
Billboard said the play "is not only remarkably alive and exciting
theatre, but provides an opportunity to witness the quiet, dignified
and sincere acting of one of our truly fine actors, Augustin Duncan.
The Guild has done a service for the theatre. . . ."[45] Robert Coleman of
the *Daily Mirror* called the production "a moving, modern Passion
play. Drinkwater tells the story with dignity, reverence and notable
dramatic impact."[46]

For the last show of the season, Blackfriars chose a play entitled
Moment Musical by Charles Angoff. Angoff, a former editor of the
American Mercury, was then in the army. The comedy concerned a
married woman from Oklahoma who comes to New York for a visit and
falls in love with a young soldier. In the end, however, she realizes it
is only infatuation and returns home to her husband. Nagle decided to
do the play because, even though the script "concerned itself with a
temptation against marital fidelity . . . its thesis fell within our
scope."[47] He explained,

> We'd use this opportunity to indicate that we were willing to come up
> against problems -- that our idea of theatre was not all sweetness and
> light. What the play was about was one thing; where the dust got in our
> eyes was in the fact that it wasn't a very good play about it.
>
> To reassure the most conservative elements in our audience, I wrote a
> program note, setting forth again our thesis and defending our choice. I
> will never write a program note again, except to clarify some minor point
> of geography or history. Most of the reviewers sunk their best barbs
> into the program note.[48]

In the program note for *Moment Musical* Father Nagle set down
what he thought the perspective of Catholic theatre should be.

Catholic theatre, like life, is not an eternally adolescent thing, built entirely on sweetness and light. People may discuss philosophy, science, temptation and sin. The only stricture imposed is that those people with whom the audience sympathetically identifies itself, must solve their problems according to the basic teaching of the Church. . . . No problem terrifies us as long as the solution is acceptable. . . .[49]

After *Moment Musical* went into rehearsal, Nagle and Carey saw an article in the *New York Times* that five theatre craft unions had blacklisted Blackfriars, along with the Provincetown Playhouse, the Malin Studio, the Heckscher Theatre and the Barbizon-Plaza Theatre. The unions stated that the "so-called experimental theatres are in reality tryout houses for legitimate producers who want to see what their untried properties look like up on stage."[50] The craft unions wanted union stage crews in all these theatres and had notified Actors Equity Association. Equity agreed, somewhat reluctantly, to forbid its members to appear in productions at these theatres. Equity, however, permitted Equity actors to remain in the cast of *Moment Musical* because the actors were unaware of the ban when they auditioned for the play.

The production of *Moment Musical* turned out to be one of Blackfriars' worst to date. George Freedley of the *Morning Telegraph* said,

we were confronted with one of the worst pieces of literary tripe that was ever shown on any stage. . . . The lines were so embarrassingly bad that you could only feel the utmost sympathy for the company and wonder how the management ever picked the play to do. A group which has offered *Savonarola* and *Song Out of Sorrow* obviously knows what it is doing, so *Moment Musical* must have been drawn blindfolded out of someone's old hat.[51]

Freedley went on to quote from Nagle's program note and observed that it would make Catholic theatre "a kind of spiritual policeman and turn its stage into something not unlike what Hollywood's Hays office would do for the screen. Show what you like so long as virtue triumphs and vice perishes."[52]

Burton Roscoe of the *World-Telegram* wrote that "Blackfriars Guild seemed so anxious to display its broadmindedness in sexual matters that it overlooked the patent fact that the play is utter trash. The play may not be immoral in the technical theological sense, but it is highly immoral aesthetically."[53]

In fact the only positive thing the reviewers had to say was about young Eileen Heckart in the supporting role of Thelma. Roscoe said "Eileen Heckart displayed great possibilities as a highly personable comedienne."[54] John B. Anderson ran Heckart's picture with his column in the *Journal-American*.[55]

Nagle was not concerned about the failure of the play. Burton Roscoe's review in the *World-Telegram* did cause him a great deal of concern. Many people, especially some Catholics, interpreted his review to mean that the Blackfriars was "broadminded in sexual matters" and that the play was "immoral." Blackfriars received letters of protest and ticket cancellations based solely on that review. Since the New York theatre was only in its second season and was striving for acceptance both outside and inside the Church, he felt that the review could be permanently damaging to Blackfriars. He wrote a four page, single-spaced letter to Roscoe, hoping perhaps for a clarification in the *World-Telegram*. Below are some excerpts from that letter,

> That you didn't like the play is of little consequence. Most of your fraternity didn't like it either, so you have support in numbers. We expect to fail now and again,. . . . But your first sentence contained a piece of uncritical journalism, which had unfortunately been accepted by those who regard the printed word as true. The consequences promise to be more serious to our efforts than even the recent arbitrary action of a few leaders of the stagehands union.

> By letter and phone we received cancellations, rebukes and sneers -- all on the head of your first sentence. . . . I categorically deny that the Blackfriars Guild is broadminded about sexual relations or that it is attempting to prove any such thesis. Perhaps the journalistic euphemism "seems" -- an invention to avoid libel suits -- takes some of the sting out of it, but the impression created among your readers remains the same. The word "broadminded" manages to imply an acceptance of that which is questionable in morality. . . .

> You did us the service of saying "the play may not be immoral in a technical theological sense but it is highly immoral esthetically. . . ." Now I'm not sure that your readers got that distinction, nor am I sure

they are to be blamed for missing precise values in the modern subjective jargon about esthetic morality. . . .

I am sure that your regard for our efforts will compel you to adjust this ridiculously false impression.[56]

The letter shows clearly that Nagle feared that Blackfriars might get a reputation in Church circles of being a liberal and broadminded organization. He was familiar with the dangers. Once before, when directing the Providence, Rhode Island Blackfriars he ran into something similar. He decided to produce Eugene O'Neill's *Days Without End* and even secured permission from O'Neill himself to produce the play without payment of royalties. He had been hesitant because, among other things, one of the characters in the play had been married previously. However he thought that the drama "solves its problem in the proper manner, even though it discusses sin."[57] There was strong negative reaction from some quarters. "Customers said they weren't coming back and the cautious grew more afraid of us. It began to look as though the process of teaching people the difference between fundamentals and accidentals -- between morality and conventions -- was going to be a difficult one," Nagle stated. "I had always expected a little opposition from the entrenched interests in the theatre in achieving our plan, but I didn't dream of the extent of the beating we'd have to take from within."[58]

There is no copy of Roscoe's letter to Nagle, but Nagle's subsequent reply indicates that it was not conciliatory.

I am sincerely sorry that my letter was subject to the same sort of misinterpretation which your review received in some places. . . .

The play was a complete mistake, I grant. The process by which I succumbed to pressure and permitted it to go on might make an interesting half hour. . . . We are trying to work out some sort of code and I thought this might be a good time to enunciate part of it. But all the while I felt we were working with the wrong vehicle.

Aside from this, your opening sentence honestly stirred up a hornet's nest. I received protests from as far away as Providence, which is a tribute to the regard in which you are held. In general they asked what sort of immorality we stood for. Confidentially, the great danger in that

attitude lies in the fact that we are more afraid of being arbitrarily closed
by Church authorities for accusations or implications of moral laxity,
than all the unions, building code and financial troubles combined. . . .

Believe me, there was no threat, veiled or otherwise, concerning libel.
What I tried to say was that even the cautious wording was generally
overlooked by the violent. Nor did I accuse you of dishonesty or
hypocrisy. It wasn't the intention of the remark which bothered me; it
was the startling effect. My letter was concerned with precision and
accuracy -- not dishonesty. . . .[59]

The letter ended with Nagle inviting Roscoe to discuss the issue
further over lunch. One assumes that they settled their differences
amicably since Roscoe not only continued to review Blackfriars but
also became one of its supporters. The incident, however, served to
illustrate the dilemma in which Blackfriars found itself. It wanted to
present drama of high quality that would appeal to mature New York
theatre-goers but also did not want to offend some of its more
parochial Catholic patrons. People who were not regular theatre-goers
and who came to Blackfriars just because it was a Catholic theatre
presented a special problem. Not only were they unsophisticated
about the theatre, some were equally unsophisticated about religious
matters and, as Nagle had stated, often confused Catholic doctrine
with social convention.

Nagle and Carey now had to turn their attention to the problem of
the crafts unions. Nagle wrote a letter to Equity objecting to including
Blackfriars with the other four theatres which were normally rented to
various producers. He pointed out that Blackfriars' charter was as an
educational and charitable institution.[60]

Obviously the reason the unions are exerting pressure is because they
are of the opinion we are acting unjustly towards their members. That
would only exist if there were non-union craftsmen profiting by our
efforts while the members of the unions were excluded, or if
shareholders, actors and other employees were receiving remuneration
while members of the crafts unions were passed by. As this is not the
case in our regard, we are sure that our status and mode of operation is
not clear to the unions and would like to present our case.

We are grateful to Equity for allowing us to continue the production
which is now in rehearsal . . . .[61]

Equity arranged a hearing and, since Nagle had to be out of town, Carey represented Blackfriars. The meeting between Carey and the Equity officials went well and they seemed sympathetic to Blackfriars. Another meeting was arranged at which members of the various theatrical crafts unions would be present. This time Nagle went to represent Blackfriars. Nagle did not have pleasant memories of that meeting:

I did everthing wrong (it was pointed out later). I used the word "blacklisting" and the "court" in a pained tone of voice said, "We don't like that word." The unhappy word had been used four times in the *Times* article and that was the sole reason we were there.

I told them how much we grossed that season. . . . I offered to show them the books. Nobody answered. So with a sense of futility, I ran off my spiel -- why we were founded, where we got our operating expenses, what we were doing for authors and actors, where we recruited our audiences. . . . And that we didn't pay anybody because we hadn't that kind of money.

Then a subdivision of the "court" spoke: "Where did you get the money to open in the first place?"

I was a little taken back at that, because the list of a few dollars here and a few dollars there would have been something to memorize. I tried to put that idea into words, but he cut in with, "You shoulda got more."[62]

The representatives of the crafts unions offered to make some concessions. Blackfriars would not have to take on a full crew -- two or three stagehands, a ticket taker, a wardrobe mistress and a press agent. Nagle responded that Blackfriars had grossed six thousand dollars for the 1942-43 season and had spent slightly more than that. The average gross for each performance was only a little over one hundred dollars. Nagle pointed out that Blackfriars could not afford to pay and added that, even if they could, they wouldn't pay stagehands unless they could also pay actors.[63]

Finally the union representatives asked what Blackfriars could afford to pay. Nagle offered to pay ten per cent of Blackfriars gross to the unions' retirement funds or other union welfare activity. The representatives did not find that offer acceptable. In a letter sent later to

Nagle they stated: "The members of the committee were of the definite opinion that your proposal 'to offer 10% of each production' and your further estimate based on your figures of last year that this amount would be about $150.00 per production could not begin to meet even the most lenient concessions possible."[64]

Blackfriars was blacklisted.

A friend of Nagle's, a union member, later told him that the unions did not believe that Blackfriars was not making money. "We were putting on shows weren't we? Then we were making money, because nobody in New York puts on shows if they aren't making money. When they stopped making money, they closed."[65]

In her column in the *Post*, Willela Waldorf came to the defense of Blackfriars. She pointed out that "for the past two seasons, Equity actors have been appearing without pay in Blackfriars productions" and she noted that several of them "have been more interesting and worth-while than the regulation Broadway product."

> Both the Studio Theatre and the Blackfriars have been giving plays that Broadway wasn't interested in, and that were in some cases better than the usual commercial product. What's going to happen to them next season is a question that should agitate all theatre-minded New Yorkers who believe that there must be some local stages open to plays that do not necessarily appeal to the business-men and their backers who run Broadway.

> No group of people is more aware of the unfortunate aspects of the situation, apparently, than the Council of the Actors Equity Association, which always moves into line with the other theatre unions, reluctantly in such cases. . . .

> Last year the Blackfriars produced four plays. . . and came out of the season in the red to the tune of $3,108, which had to be raised by passing the hat among its patrons. But it is apparently difficult to convince the various craft unions that anybody can possibly be doing anything in the theatre without the intention of making money. . . .[66]

After the official and final "blacklisting," Nagle especially worried about the reaction of Blackfriars' patrons, especially the clergy, many of whom were supporters of the unions. He decided to write a letter to the priests of the area. In this "Confidential Report to Our Friends

Among the Clergy" he defended Blackfriars and pointed out that the theatre was not anti-union. It simply could not function if forced to pay union wages -- "where it cost $6,000 to operate, with union set up it would have cost $60,000 to operate."[67] He closed the letter by asking for the priests' continued support.

Blackfriars began the 1943-44 season knowing that they would be unable to use Equity actors in their shows. Of course, it presented problems. One young actor got a commercial acting job while in rehearsal for a Blackfriars production. The schedule of the two shows did not conflict, but the commercial play required him to join Equity which meant that he had to quit the Blackfriars production.

The 1943-44 season, however, turned out to be the success that Nagle and Carey needed to boost their morale after the dismal 1942-43 season. The first production was *Career Angel*, a comedy-fantasy written by Father Gerard M. Murray, assistant pastor at Our Lady of Mercy Church in Forest Hills, New York. Murray set the play in a financially troubled orphanage run by a group of Brothers. The complications centered around a guardian angel, visible only to one Brother, and a group of Nazi spies. Nagle contacted Cardinal Hayes High School for Boys and cast several of its students as the orphans. Veteran actor Liam Dunn, who had been in *Up the Rebels* and *Savonarola*, appeared as Brother Gregory.

The press was lavish in its praise of the production. Burton Roscoe of the *World-Telegram* wrote,

> Hold everything! ... Believe it or not, one of the wittiest, most intellectually satisfying, most refreshing comedies that has been produced in New York in years is to be seen at the Blackfriars Theatre.... If *The Naked Genius* [Gypsy Rose Lee's autobiography] is worth the $350,000 which Hollywood paid for it, this play is worth more money than the national debt.[68]

Willela Waldorf of the *Post* said: "Last night found the company [Blackfriars] in one of its more antic moods. ... When they go in for comedy they believe in laughing without being prissy. Some of the angel's cracks, in fact, got more laughs than Milton Berle."[69] *Cue* magazine stated: "*Career Angel* is a blithe and amusing fantasy about faith in one's guardian angel. Despite its comedy and amusement, it is basically something challenging and provocative. ...."[70] Roy Barrett of the *Daily News* called *Career Angel* "a literate, almost poetic work . . . a wandering playgoer might well spend an interesting evening over on 57th Street."[71] Robert Coleman of the *Daily Mirror* thought that "with a good rewrite, slicker staging and a professional cast, it would tower head and shoulders over most of the tenants of our Broadway theatres."[72]

The play enjoyed such success that it had to be held over for extra performances, giving it a run of four weeks. George Jean Nathan included *Career Angel* in his list of outstanding plays for the 1943-44 season.[73] Burton Roscoe called *Career Angel* New York's best play of the year.[74]

Broadway immediately picked up *Career Angel*. The revised play opened at the National Theatre on May 23, 1944. It was not, however, a success. Professional child actors replaced the natural-acting amateurs from Cardinal Hayes High School and the slickness of the production appears to have hurt the simplicity and freshness of the play. Rowland Field of the *Newark News* said: "Curiously enough, the play seems to have lost some of its fanciful appeal during alterations in transit, nor is the current Equity cast generally as effective . . . as the original company."[75] Though not a Broadway success, *Career Angel* was the first Off-Broadway play ever to move to Broadway.[76] Dramatists Play Service published *Career Angel* for amateur production.

The next production was a play entitled *Caukey*, written by Father Thomas McGlynn, O.P., a priest who was primarily a sculptor. Father McGlynn knew something about the theatre because he was the son of actor Frank McGlynn who was famous for playing the lead role in John Drinkwater's *Abraham Lincoln*. The younger McGlynn had also been a child actor in silent movies. Though McGlynn spent much of his time carving religious statues, he had worked for a while in a black settlement house in Chicago and had become concerned about the plight of African-Americans. This concern resulted in his play, *Caukey*, which he based on the premise of what might happen if the black race were in the majority and the Caucasian race an oppressed minority. McGlynn portrayed the blacks as rich and powerful, the whites as an underprivileged minority barred from decent housing, schools and jobs. "Caukey" was a pejorative term for whites used by the blacks. The drama centered on the efforts of one intelligent, but poor white boy to get ahead in a black-dominated society. The script called for African-Americans to be "planted" in the audience and to heckle the white actors on stage.

Blackfriars knew it would have difficulty casting the play because it required a dozen good black actors who had to be non-Equity. Father Nagle contacted the American Negro Theatre and they agreed to provide the black actors in exchange for co-sponsorship of the play. Therefore *Caukey* became a joint production of the Blackfriars Guild and the American Negro Theatre. The play opened on February 17, 1944 with actress Ruth White playing the mother of the struggling young white man.[77] Burton Roscoe stated,

The Blackfriars have done it again! *Caukey* . . . is a soul wrenching, hard-hitting, searingly sardonic and ironical arraignment of race prejudice . . . . It nearly tore my heart out, so poignant is the drama of it, which, in anguish and in sorrow, points a severely accusing finger at me and at you . . . . It is a merciless indictment from which no one . . . can wholly escape, for it is an indictment of our little unconscious and falsely conditioned reflex actions in violation of the spirit of the brotherhood of man as well as those of more vicious violations of the spirit which are prompted by greed, selfishness, arrogance, vanity and an inveterate deficiency in our sense of justice.

If you are weary of the nice, tailor-made formula plays, the adroit smart comedies and the clever machine-made farces of Broadway, go and see *Caukey* -- if you can get in. . . .[78]

Robert Coleman wrote that, "*Caukey* is not a play for the commercial theatre, but it is an interesting play, a play that merits a hearing and the Blackfriars Guild is to be commended for its courage in presenting a script that might not otherwise have gained a sponsor."[79] Kelsey Allen of *Women's Wear Daily* reported: "Last night he [McGlynn] proved that he is also an excellent playwright. He has a fine control of language, a good sense of theatre and his future work for the stage should find a real market."[80] Jack O'Brien of the Associated Press thought that "the prologue and the first act were among the most exciting minutes I have experienced in the theatre."[81]

Other critics were less enthusiastic about the play. John Chapman said McGlynn "has a better idea than a play. . . . However, Father McGlynn has managed to be shocking in the mere simplicity of his notion . . . . *Caukey* isn't a play by good professional standards, but it isn't a soapbox speech either. It makes its points with dignity if not with complete skill, and the points are obviously worth making."[82]

At least three black reviewers covered the production of *Caukey*. The reviewer for the black publication, the *Pittsburgh Courier*, called the play "an earnest plea for better racial understanding." The *Courier* went on to say that, "although it probably came as a shock to the white members of the audience, maybe not an agreeable one, the small things which are so familiar to the Negroes of the audience were glaringly outstanding when applied to white people."[83] George Heath of the *People's Voice*, a New York black newspaper, thought *Caukey* produced "hilarious and grim results. *Caukey* finally emerges as a rough-hewn social drama about racial injustices. It says nothing new or newly to the Negro, but its serves to make whites squirm."[84] Black columnist Geraldyn Desmond of the Independent Press Service wrote, after seeing the play: "Little theatre groups would do well to follow the example of the Blackfriars Guild and let White America put itself in the place of Black America for an evening. The mental gymnastics would do a lot of smug people a world of good."[85] There was a strong negative reaction, however, from one Southern newspaper. The *Tampa* (Florida) *Sunday Tribune* called the play "an emphatically offensive contribution to racial controversy." The newspaper reported that "the reaction to the play by audiences and critics has been one of shocked revulsion" and predicted the production "will intensify racial feeling. Responsibility for the play rests upon Father McGlynn, the Blackfriars Guild and the American Negro Theatre."[86]

Despite a few negative reviews, Father Nagle was extremely pleased with the production of *Caukey*. It was a successful production and the kind of play that he thought made their Catholic theatre venture worthwhile.

> As a result of *Caukey*, the Negroes in Chicago or Harlem or Detroit or Philadelphia haven't suddenly had restrictive covenants lifted. But that's hardly what the author set out to achieve. If legislation, welfare workers, missionaries and the understandable ambition of a great Negro minority in this country have settled so few problems since the Emancipation Proclamation, it is not surprising that this play hasn't settled them. It did offer a jolt to prejudice and it did set up the only pattern by which they can be solved.[87]

The enthusiasm engendered by *Career Angel* and *Caukey* gave Nagle and Carey a new lease of hope. "We were being talked about from Tampa to Kansas City," said Nagle. "Our friends were growing in numbers and becoming articulate. A large section of the press was openly pulling for us. . . ."[88]

Since negotiations with Equity and doubts about whether or not they could use union actors caused a delay in beginning the season --*Career Angel* didn't open until mid-November -- Blackfriars could only produce three plays during the 1943-44 season. For their last show they produced *Earth Journey* by Sheldon Davis. It was a fable, set in China, about a statue that comes to life and falls in love with a princess. The play made use of Chinese staging techniques and a brief explanation of Chinese theatre appeared in the program. Director Dennis Gurney appeared as the property man who addresses the audience. John Chapman of the *Daily News* said the play was "the kind of prose which should be reviewed by the Bureau of Weights and Measures," and added that it "must have been written as a penance."[89]

For the first time Blackfriars ended the season with a slight profit -- $238.62.[90] Production expenses totaled $9,611.33 -- the theatre was still not paying any salaries. Total ticket sales came to $9,199.95 and donations from friends and benefactors came to $650.00.

In the 1944-45 season the theatre group went back to producing four plays. The season was not as dismal as 1942-43, nor as successful as 1943-44. The first play was an innocuous comedy called *Don't George* by Katherine Laure. The program note for *Don't George* carried a notice from Mayor LaGuardia about what to do in case of an air raid.

Home is the Hero by Courtney Savage was the second production. It concerned a returning serviceman who finds his wife making more money that he can hope to start making and the consequent family problems. Savage had previously had six plays produced in New York, none of them critical successes. *Home is the Hero* was only mildly successful.

For the Lenten season, Blackfriars chose to do *Simon's Wife* by Father Francis D. Alwaise, O.P. The play concerned the chagrin and bewilderment of Simon Peter's wife, Leah, when her husband leaves his family and fishing trade to become leader of the Apostles. The critic for the *Herald-Tribune* commented that "even for a morality play, *Simon's Wife* is naively outlined with wooden characters and talky situations and . . . is stiffly acted."[91]

The season closed with Blackfriars' first attempt at a musical, *Slice It Thin,* with book and lyrics by Lieutenant Edward N. Heghinian and music by Al Moritz. Moritz had previously written songs for Ethel Waters' revue, "Blue Holiday." Lewis Nichols thought the play was "a good deal like a commencement show" and commented that "it will do no one any lasting harm."[92]

Blackfriars had now completed four seasons in New York and in that short time had acquired an excellent reputation among theatre people, especially the drama critics who regularly reviewed Blackfriars productions. Robert Coleman of the *Daily Mirror* wrote,

> The Blackfriars Guild is New York's number one experimental theatre. It has introduced several new playwrights of promise and brought a number of gifted young players to the attention of Broadway managers. Actors Equity and the Legion of New York Theatres should encourage the formation of other such groups in greater New York. They develop new talent and new audiences for the commercial theatre.[93]

Willela Waldorf of the *Post* said, "Blackfriars' plays generally have something to say, and even if they don't say it brilliantly, they're likely to be more interesting than many of the goings-on farther south in the vicinity of Times Square."[94] Jack O'Brien of the Associated Press commented: "With all its shortcomings, it is evident that the Blackfriars must be given a maximum of attention whenever they offer a play."[95] And Kelsey Allen of *Women's Wear Daily* called Blackfriars "the most important of our several experimental playhouses."[96]

1. Urban Nagle, O.P., MS "The Catholic Theatre," n.d., Nagle papers, Dominican Archives, Washington, D.C., 1.

2. Urban Nagle, O.P., MS "My Dear Blackfriars," n.d., Nagle papers, 3.

3. Urban Nagle, O.P., *Behind the Masque* (New York: McMullen Books, Inc.), 135.

4. Ibid., 140.

5. Ibid., 160.

6. Program, *Daddy Come Home* by Rose Grieco, 16 April-26 May 1963, Blackfriars Collection, Providence College Archives, Providence, R.I.

7. Jerry Evans, interview by author, telephone, 19 May 1983. Evans is former director for Blackfriars.

8. Nagle, the Catholic Theatre, 3.

9. Urban Nagle, O.P., MS "The Philosophy of Art and the Catholic Theatre Movement," Nagle papers, 2.

10. Ibid.

11. Nagle, *Behind the Masque*, 141.

12. Ibid., 137-138.

13. Ibid., 140.

14. Ibid., 140-141.

15. Father Brendan Larnen, O.P., interview by author, 12 May 1983.

16. Dennis Gurney, typewritten resume, Blackfriars Collection.

17. Nagle, *Behind the Masque*, 157.

18. Geraldine Page, interview by author, 10 October 1982.

19. Nagle, *Behind the Masque*, 143.

20. Ibid., 145.

21. Ibid., 151.

22. Liam Dunn became a character actor in films and television. His films include *Young Frankenstein* and *What's Up, Doc?*

23. Louis Calta, "Up The Rebels," *New York Times*, 31 October 1941.

24. Bide Dudley, Review, WHN Radio, 30 October 1941, Blackfriars Collection.

25. Ben Bradford, "Song Out of Sorrow Given," *New York Times*, 12 December 1941.

26. Robert Francis, "Song Out of Sorrow," *The Brooklyn Eagle*, 12 December 1941.

27. Nagle, *Behind the Masque*, 165.

28. Stuart W. Little, *Off-Broadway: The Prophetic Theatre* (New York: Coward, McCann & Geoghegan, Inc., 1972), 37-38

29. Brookes, Atkinson, "Uncle Pete Fixes Everything," *New York Times*, 7 February 1942.

30. Nagle, *Behind the Masque*, 173.

31. Robert Coleman, "*Savonarola* is Study of Churchman," *New York Daily Mirror*, 24 April 1942.

32. Robert Sylvester, "*Savonarola* Offered," *New York Daily News*, 24 April 1942.

33. Richard Watts, "The Theatre," *New York Herald-Tribune*, 9 August 1942.

34. Financial statement, 1941-1942, typewritten sheet, Blackfriars Collection.

35. Nagle, *Behind the Masque*, 180.

36. Ibid.

37. Ibid., 181.

38. Joseph Pihodna, "Inside Story," *New York Herald-Tribune*, 30 October 1942.

39. Lewis Nichols, "Blackfriars Fantasy," *New York Times*, 29 January 1943.

40. Eileen Heckart later appeared in *Moment Musical* at Blackfriars. She appeared on Broadway in *Picnic*, *The Bad Seed*, *A View From the Bridge*, *The Dark at the Top of the Stairs*, *Everybody Loves Opal*, *Barefoot in the Park*, *You Know I Can't Hear You When the Water's Running*, *Butterflies Are Free*, *The Effect of Gamma Rays on Man-in-the-Moon Marigolds*, and *Veronica's Room*. Her films include *Miracle in the Rain*, *The Bad Seed*, *Bus Stop* and *Butterflies Are Free*. She received an NATAS (Emmy) Award for her performance in *Save Me a Place at Forest Lawn* and an Academy Award for best supporting actress for *Butterflies Are Free*.

41. Burns Mantle, "Tinker's Dam," *New York Daily News* 29 January 1943. Dort Clark, mentioned in the review, went on to appear in several Broadway productions, mainly musicals. He had featured roles in the original productions of *South Pacific*, *Wonderful Town*, *Bells Are Ringing*, *Take Me Along* and *Fiorello*.

42. Willela Waldorf, "Two on the Aisle," *New York Post*, 29 January 1943.

43. Cavada Humphrey subsequently appeared in many Broadway and regional productions as well as films. She is probably best known for appearing with her husband, Jerome Kilty, in *Dear Liar*.

44. Mimeographed press release, n.d., Nagle papers.

45. Shirley Frolich, "Blackfriars Scored With *Man's House*," *Billboard*, 24 April 1943.

46. Robert Coleman, "The Theatre," *New York Daily Mirror*, 5 April 1943.

47. Nagle, *Behind the Masque*, 186.

48. Ibid., 186-187.

49. Program, *Moment Musical* by Charles Angoff, 31 May-12 June 1943, Blackfriars Collection.

50. "Unions Not to Block Show by Blackfriars," *New York Times*, 27 May 1943.

51. George Freedley, "The Stage Today," *New York Morning Telegraph*, 1

June 1943.

52. Ibid.

53. Burton Roscoe, "The Theatre," *New York World-Telegram*, 1 June 1932.

54. Ibid.

55. John Anderson, "Theatre," *New York Journal-American*, 1 June 1943.

56. Urban Nagle, O.P., to Burton Roscoe, 5 June 1943, Nagle papers.

57. Nagle, *Behind the Masque*, 81.

58. Ibid.

59. Urban Nagle, O.P., to Burton Roscoe, n.d., Nagle papers.

60. The Blackfriars Guild of America had been incorporated "for the education in and promotion of the arts" in Washington, D.C. on 13 October 1936. A copy of the articles of incorporation is in the Blackfriars Collection.

61. Urban Nagle, O.P., to Paul Dulzell, executive secretary of Actors Equity Association, 26 May 1943, Nagle papers.

62. Nagle, *Behind the Masque*, 190.

63. Ibid., 191.

64. Ibid., 192.

65. Ibid.

66. Willela Waldorf, "Two on the Aisle," *New York Post*, 29 May 1943.

67. Urban Nagle, "Confidential Report to Our Friends Among the Clergy," n.d., Nagle papers.

68. Burton Roscoe, "The Theatre," *New York World-Telegram*, 19 November 1943.

69. Willela Waldorf, "Two on the Aisle," *New York Post*, 19 November 1943.

70. *Cue*, 24 November 1943.

71. Roy Barrett, "Blackfriars Return With Well Written Tale of Gay Angel," *New York Daily News*, 19 November 1943.

72. Robert Coleman, "*Career Angel* Both Original, Pleasing," *New York Daily Mirror*, 19 November 1943.

73. George Jean Nathan, "Several Plays Worth Awards Last Season," *New York Journal-American*, 22 May 1944.

74. Catherine Hughes, "Show Business Showcase," *Ave Maria*, 13 June 1959, 7.

75. Rowland Field, "Broadway," *Newark News*, 24 May 1944.

76. Robert Louis Hobbs, "Off-Broadway: The Early Years," Diss. Northwestern University 1964., 22.

77. Ruth White appeared on Broadway in *The Ponder Heart*, *The Happiest Millionaire*, *Rashomon*, *The Warm Peninsula*, *Whisper to Me*, *Big Fish/Little Fish*, *Lord Pengo*, and *Absence of a Cello*. Her films include *The Nun's Story*, *Charly* and *To Kill a Mockingbird*. She won an NATAS (Emmy) Award for *Little Moon of Alban* and an Obie (*Village Voice* Off-Broadway) Award for

her role in Samuel Beckett's *Happy Days*.

78. Burton Roscoe, "The Theatre," *New York World-Telegram*, 18 February 1944.

79. Robert Coleman, "The Theatre," *New York Daily Mirror*, 18 February 1944.

80. Kelsey Allen, "Caukey," *Women's Wear Daily*, 18 February 1944.

81. Jack O'Brien, Associated Press dispatch, 26 February 1944, Blackfriars Collection.

82. John Chapman, "Suppose the Negroes Ran Things," *New York Daily News*, 19 February 1944.

83. "Izzy," "Play Presents A New Approach to Racial Problems," *Pittsburgh Courier*, 26 February 1944.

84. George Health, "Caucasians Put on Spot by Priest in Blackfriars' New Production," *The People's Voice*, 26 February 1944.

85. Geraldyn Desmond, "Gerldyn Desmond Says," Independent Press Service, March 1944, Blackfriars Collection.

86. *Tampa (Florida) Sunday Tribune*, 27 February 1944.

87. Nagle, *Behind the Masque*, 201-202.

88. Ibid., 206.

89. John Chapman, "Blackfriars' New Play Has Chinese Blah," *New York Daily News*, 28 April 1944.

90. Financial statement 1943-1944, Blackfriars Collection. All financial information in this paragraph is from this typewritten sheet.

91. O.L.G., "Simon's Wife," *New York Herald-Tribune*, 9 March 1945.

92. Lewis Nichols, "With Music" *New York Times*, 11 May 1945.

93. Robert Coleman, "The Theatre," *New York Daily Mirror*, 5 April 1943.

94. Willela Waldorf, "Two on the Aisle," *New York Post*, 18 February 1944.

95. Jack O'Brien, Associated Press Dispatch, 26 February 1944, Blackfriars collection.

96. Kelsey Allen, "Caukey," *Women's Wear Daily*, 18 February 1944.

CHAPTER 3
GROWTH AND CONTROVERSY: 1945-1952

In the years 1945-1952 Blackfriars experienced considerable growth. Blackfriars played its productions seven evenings a week for an average four week run. This is compared to the four performances of their first play, *Up the Rebels*. Some productions, like *Lady of Fatima* in 1948, *City of Kings* in 1949 and *Armor of Light* in 1950 (all three by Father Nagle), played for eight weeks. Ticket prices also increased. For the 1948-49 season tickets cost $2.40, $1.80, and $1.20.[1] Preview matinees for Catholic sisters, which had been done before, now became an established part of the run of a play. They were dress rehearsals on the Saturday and Sunday before the opening. The sisters, who comprised the entire audience, paid no admission.

During this period also the group of laymen and women who had previously been informal sponsors of Blackfriars formed themselves into the Blackfriars Auxiliary. This group primarily sponsored fund-raising events such as card parties and dances. The profits from these events helped Blackfriars to operate in the black, though box office office receipts still remained the theatre's major source of income.

Blackfriars began at this time to develop an extensive mailing list in order to reach its regular subscribers. Another ticket promotion instituted in these years was the theatre party. Blackfriars encouraged Catholic parishes and organizations to buy blocks of seats by offering a rebate to the parish or organization. For example, if a parish group purchased seventy-eight seats, $17.10 was returned as a profit. This plan, however, caused Blackfriars to depend more and more on parish groups for its audiences. Already in 1948 Father Nagle wrote that "our audiences are not drawn from the regular theatre. They are for the most part promoted from parish societies by written appeals to priest moderators. They are a movie audience. The theatre people who attend are our guests. I should be very surprised," Nagle speculated, "if ten per cent of our audiences saw three commercial productions a year."[2]

Blackfriars' role as a showcase for young actors increased. In 1948 Nagle estimated that more than a hundred actors in Blackfriars productions had found work in the professional theatre and become Equity members.[3] Also the controversy with Equity had begun to fade from people's memories and many Equity actors were appearing in Blackfriars productions using assumed names. This was apparently done with the tacit permission of Equity officials, at least those who were still aware of the "ban" on Blackfriars.

Scene designers during this period worked on a per-production basis. A number of designers worked for Blackfriars, but three designed frequently. Avril Gentles, a free-lance designer who had previously designed *Career Angel*, designed *Come Marching Home*, *Derryowen*, *If in the Greenwood* and *On the Seventh Day*.[4] David Reppa, a graduate of the Goodman School of Drama in Chicago and formerly designer at the Bucks County Playhouse in Pennsylvania, designed *Respectfully Yours*, *Hoboes in Heaven*, *Lady of Fatima* and *Minstrel Boy*. And Floyd Allen, who had a degree in design from the Pasadena Playhouse School of Theatre and had designed for five years in Hollywood and two years at the Goodman Theatre in Chicago, did sets for *City of Kings*, *Angel With Red Hair*, and *Open the Gates*.

Father Nagle continued to manage Blackfriars and during the 1945-52 period wrote four plays for Blackfriars and co-authored another. Nagle's interests, however, widened to include radio and the pioneer medium of television. In 1944 Nagle had become a regular personality on the "Hour of Faith" national radio program. Toward the end of the decade he was frequently appearing on television. He also wrote two books popular with Catholic readers--*Uncle George and Uncle Malachy* in 1946, a series of humorous but pointed stories about two uncles who discuss religion; and *Behind the Masque* in 1951, an anecdotal history of his twenty years in the Catholic theatre movement.[5] The priest was also in demand as a lecturer, preacher and after-dinner speaker.

Carey continued to work, as he had done previously, behind the scenes. He concerned himself with promotion, fund-raising and the building of sets. Using the name Thomas Fabian, he had even designed the set for *Caukey*. He was also still assigned to full-time work on the *Holy Name Journal*. However, during this period a conflict would develop between Nagle and Carey over finances and the direction of Blackfriars.

A disagreement at the Holy Name Society, where Father Nagle was offically assigned, ironically allowed him to work full-time at Blackfriars. A letter of Nagle's to Father Henry C. Graham, O.P., director of the Holy Name Society, during the summer of 1945, indicates a conflict between the two priests over Nagle's role in Blackfriars. In the letter Nagle apparently defends himself against charges that he spent too much time away from the Holy Name office and that he was using Holy Name staff and equipment for Blackfriars' business. It is also apparent from the letter that Nagle was attempting to perform two full-time jobs.[6] Soon after, on October 18, Nagle received a letter from Father Terence S. McDermott, provincial superior of the Dominicans of the Province of Saint Joseph, relieving him of all his duties at the *Holy Name Journal* and assigning him full-time, "at least for the present," to the work of the Blackfriars.[77] However, in the process, McDermott moved Nagle from Saint Vincent Ferrer Priory at Lexington Avenue and Sixty-fifth Street where he had been living to Sacred Heart Priory in Jersey City. Fr. McDermott's transfer of Nagle to Sacred Heart may indicate that there was at least some degree of animosity between Nagle and Fr. Graham, who also lived at St. Vincent Ferrer. Perhaps McDermott wanted to separate them completely. Residing in Jersey City meant two long subway rides for Nagle each day.

The first play that Blackfriars produced in the 1945-46 season had a large number of authors. *Seven Mirrors* resulted from a student drama project at Immaculate Heart College in Los Angeles. Ten young women, working under the supervision of playwright Emmet Lavery, had produced this play which they called "an experiment in social drama." The play dealt with the state of the world and woman's part in it and was divided into seven episodes in seven different locations. A different Madonna figure appeared in each episode. It called for a cast of eleven men and thirty women and made use of music and dance.

Otis Guernsey of the *Herald-Tribune* wrote that "its thinking edge is blunted with cliches, and its general theme, the combination of religion and living, is anything but subtle."[8] The cast included young actresses Geraldine Page as a college junior and Patricia Neal as "first volunteer."[9] Miss Page got a favorable mention in Robert Coleman's review in the *Daily Mirror*.[10] Neal left the cast of *Seven Mirrors* to become an understudy in *The Voice of the Turtle*, then in its fourth year on Broadway. *Seven Mirrors* was later published for amateur performance by Samuel French, Inc.

Blackfriars' next play, its second one to treat the problem of racial prejudice, was *A Young American*, written by Edwin M. Bronner, music and drama critic for WWRL radio in New York. It told the story of an orchestra conductor who receives an excellent score for a symphony through the mail from a young composer. The conductor invites the composer, a music student at a southern university, to spend the rehearsal weeks with him in his home in New York to smooth out the composition. When the composer arrives the conductor and his family discover for the first time that the young man is black. The conductor tries to adapt himself to the situation and make the young composer feel at home. Complications set in when the maid quits because she will not serve a "nigger" and the suitor of the conductor's daughter objects to the composer's presence in the house. The composer is shocked and embittered by the treatment he receives. However, his elderly black music teacher comes in at a critical moment and offers the young man some sound advice on dealing with racial prejudice.

Blackfriars cast Louis Peterson, Jr. in the role of the young composer.[11] Peterson, a young African-American actor who had attended the Yale Drama School, was also an accomplished pianist. Another young actor, Sidney Poitier, auditioned for the role but was turned down because of his inability to play the piano.

The reviewer for *Variety* called it "a poignant plea for racial tolerance adeptly handled in context and admirably enacted by the competent cast under the nifty directorial guidance of Dennis Gurney."[12] He added that "Louis Peterson Jr. plays the Negro with restraint and poise" and said that "with a professional production it might do on the main stem." Robert Coleman of the *Daily Mirror* wrote that "Dennis Gurney has capably directed a cast that acts the play with the same intensity and conviction that Bronner had displayed in the writing."[13] Coleman pointed out that "it is a script that in its present form might not be considered commercial by many Broadway managers. So it is a fine thing indeed to have an organization like the Blackfriars to give young, idealistic dramatists like Bronner the hearing that is often denied them by the professional managers further downtown."

Producer Lee Shubert picked up the play almost immediately and arranged for a pre-Broadway tryout in Chicago. Several other producers had also expressed interest in the play. Shubert arranged for Albert de Courville to direct. Blackfriars closed *A Young American* on February 11, 1946 and the Shubert production opened fifteen days later at the Great Northern Theatre in Chicago with a partially new cast and a few hasty script changes. William Greaves played the black composer. The fact that Greaves could not play the piano proved to be a major drawback for the production.

The Shubert production received a mixed response from Chicago critics and audiences. Robert Casey of the *Chicago News* wrote that the play had "courage and honesty." He added, however, that "what's in store for it, we shouldn't care to prophesy. It may make people think, and we lack the statistics on the percentage of local show-goers willing to expose their brains to a draft."[14] However, Claudia Cassidy of the *Chicago Tribune* called it "a poor play which brings up a controversial subject without clarifying its problems."[15] Cassidy pointed out that the lead couldn't play the piano and said that the piano reproduction "sounds like a tin pan being beaten." Lack of critical support and audiences caused the production to close in Chicago after only twelve performances.

After the production of *Simon's Wife* during the Lent of 1945 and its response from Catholic audiences, Nagle wanted to do another specifically religious play for the Lenten season. He wanted a play "about actable, approachable, entirely human characters, real or fictitious (in the sense of representatives for the rest of us), showing the influence of Christ's coming among us."[16] He found such a script in *Mary of Magdala* by Ernest Milton, an American actor who had spent much of his life in England. The play presented Mary Magdalene as the popular hostess of the *demi-monde* of Jerusalem and friend of the Romans who eventually finds faith in Jesus.

For its spring production Blackfriars fortunately found *Come Marching Home*, the first play by young playwright Robert

Anderson.[17] Anderson had written the play while he was a naval lieutenant aboard the cruiser *Alaska* during World War II. The play won first prize in the National Theatre Conference's contest in 1944 as the best play written by an American serviceman overseas. The University of Iowa had produced the play in 1945 and Anderson was eager for a New York production. *Come Marching Home* told the story of a naval hero who consents to run for state senator in opposition to the ruthless boss of a corrupt political machine. Soon the hero's opponents have smeared his character and even his own party deserts him the night before the election. He stays in the race as an independent, however, and though he faces a certain defeat he promises to come back in succeeding campaigns to rouse the public to its civic duty.

Drama critic George Freedley thought that *Come Marching Home* was "one of the most worthwhile Blackfriars productions in several seasons."[18] Kelsey Allen said: "Mr. Anderson writes with an unusual touch of intelligence and his character drawing is excellent."[19] "Though *Come Marching Home* is a sincere, honest, impassioned play," said Robert Coleman, "it will hardly reach Broadway or as wide an audience as it merits."[20] Coleman praised Blackfriars for producing the play and wrote,

> The Blackfriars Guild has given first hearings to a number of gifted playwrights in the last five years and Anderson is one of the best. We only wish there were dozens of experimental theatres like it hereabouts to encourage and introduce new writing and acting talents.

A few critics, however, thought that the play fell short of its potential. *Variety*'s critic called the play "a sincere effort that should rate attention and an extended run," but said "it's hardly sturdy enough for Broadway."[21] Otis Guernsey, Jr. thought that

> the play's chief fault is that of occasionally mistaking the stage for a soap box, an error all too common among those who have something important to say. When the hero is coming to grips with his opponents or his own conscience, there is drama on the Blackfriars stage; but too many lines seem to be coming direct from the writer to the audience without detouring through the characters.[22]

Because of the production of *Come Marching Home*, the *New York*

Post did a feature article on Anderson, with photographs of him and his wife, and called him "a promising playwright."[23]

Anderson later recalled, "It was a fine experience: play written, play produced, play appraised by the regular critics."[24] Anderson went on to a successful career as a playwright and screenwriter.

Records indicate that Blackfriars ended the 1945-46 season $250.00 in the black.[25] The records also show that Gurney was paid a salary of roughly a thousand dollars for directing four plays. Merritt Wyatt, the financial and box office manager, earned a salary of $1,200.

During the summer of 1946 the staff drew up a budget for the 1946-47 season. It included a salary of $1,500 for Gurney, $1,500 for Wyatt, $1,500 for Bill Schoeller, the technical director and general carpenter, and $1,200 for a secretary. For the first time a salary was paid to Father Nagle, who was no longer working on the *Holy Name Journal* and was now working full-time at Blackfriars. He would receive a salary of $2,000. The budget also included another $1,000 as the capital needed to start the following season. The proposed budget was as follows:

Salaries	$7,700
Rent	2,970
Taxes	4,000
Telephone	300
Promotions	600
Printing	1,000
Advertisements	400
Productions ($300 each)	1,200
Parties for cast	200
Cleaning, elevator service	500
Blackfriars Guild (capital for next season)	*1,000*
TOTAL	$19,870

An addendum to the budget also stated that, in the event of a "profit" after the above expenses had been paid, Gurney, Wyatt and Schoeller were to be paid a bonus. It also indicated that, except for small incidental expenses, Nagle's salary was to be paid directly to his religious superior. Father Carey, still working on the *Holy Name Journal*, received no salary from Blackfriars.

A newspaper story which amused Father Brendan Larnen, O.P. provided the basis for Blackfriars' opening play for 1946-47. Larnen, who had written Blackfriars' first play, had read a news item during the Second World War which caused him to chuckle and which he kept in the back of his mind as a possible basis for a comedy. The British government, perhaps in an effort to entice Ireland into the war, had issued a press release which stated that there were 300 Japanese in Ireland disguised as Irishmen. Father Larnen finally wrote the comedy, entitled *Derryowen*, under the pen name Michael O'Hara. The comedy, set in a pub on the Irish seacoast during World War II, dealt with the efforts of an American correspondent to find the Japanese "spies" and the reaction of the local populace. Former vaudevillian Gerald Buckley, who had appeared in the original company of *Shadow and Substance*, played the Irish pub keeper and King Donovan appeared as the correspondent.[26] The reviewer for *Billboard*, unaware that "Mr. O'Hara" was a priest, wrote that "while he [O'Hara] has a lot to learn about writing love scenes, he does manage to work in considerable chuckles via some earthy, amusing dialog."[27]

One of the people who saw *Derryowen* was Clarence Derwent, the president of the Actors Equity Association. He talked with Father Nagle in the lobby during intermission and acknowledged that he had been unaware that Equity members were forbidden to appear in Blackfriars' shows and suggested that Nagle present Blackfriars' case again to the Council of Equity. Nagle later wrote a lengthy letter to Derwent, thanking him for his suggestion, but said "I'd almost rather struggle along as we have done than face the humiliation of a repetition of the last appeal."[28]

Blackfriars next production was an unfortunate selection, *If in the Greenwood* by Victoria Kuhn. Kuhn had written the play while on a Dinneen Playwrighting Fellowship at Rosary College, sponsored by the National Catholic Theatre Conference. The play concerned the dilemma of a man of ability and integrity who is nominated as a delegate to the United Nations. His rival attempts to blackmail him because of the suicide of his wife and her platonic lover. The play was written in blank verse and neither the audiences nor the critics liked the play.

The Lenten season was now approaching and Blackfriars, wanting to keep its tradition of presenting an overtly religious play for Lent, needed a script. Father Nagle decided to finish a play he had been working on for some time. The play was *On the Seventh Day*, a drama about angels watching, commenting and acting on the problems of the human family. The central figure among the humans is a disillusioned returned war veteran. Darren McGavin appeared in the role of the young veteran. McGavin had previously appeared in small parts in four films and, as a member of the Screen Actors Guild, he had to appear at Blackfriars under an assumed name. McGavin used the name Mel York, a shortened form of his first wife's name, Melanie York.[29] The play was a change of pace from Nagle's previous writing because in this play he made use of expressionistic techniques.

The play did not receive a good press, as is exemplified in the title of William Hawkin's review in the *World-Telegram* -- "Tired Archangel in a Tiresome Drama."[30] The reviewers did have favorable things to say about York/McGavin, however.

Blackfriars closed the 1946-47 season with *Respectfully Yours* by Peggy Lamson, a free lance writer and the wife of a Williams College English professor. The play was a nostalgic comedy, set in 1912, about the timid wife of a stuffy Harvard professor who writes a book about assertiveness for women. The play had previously been produced at the Dock Street Theatre in Charleston, South Carolina with Dorothy Gish playing the lead. It had been bought by the Theatre Guild, but never produced. Marjorie Hildreth directed the production, the first that Gurney had not staged. Hildreth had studied at the Pasadena Playhouse and had previously directed for the Equity Theatre Library and the American Negro Theatre, as well as in summer stock.[31] Though the play never did make it to Broadway, the Blackfriars production did get nine good reviews from the critics.

During the summer of 1947 the theatre was redecorated. Critic Robert Coleman made note of the changes in the fall: "It [Blackfriars] is now an even more pleasant place to spend an evening, seeing plays that Broadway thinks it cannot afford to produce."[32]

Over the summer a few ex-servicemen who were friends of Nagle's told him about a play they had seen in Paris, *Les Gueux aux Paradis* by G.M. Martens and Andre Obey. Nagle secured a copy of the script and had Robert Healey, a former student of his at Providence College, translate it. Efforts to contact the authors in France to secure permission to produce the play were unsuccessful. Finally Nagle contacted the French Embassy and when even the French Embassy could not get a response, the Embassy told Nagle that it would take full responsibility and to proceed with the production which opened the 1947-48 season.[33]

The play relates the story of a Flemish innkeeper and his friend who every year on the eve of Saint Nicholas Day dress as Saint Nicholas and Saint Nicodemus and distribute toys and sweets to the children of the village. One year, however, they are nearly killed by an automobile and, while they are unconscious, tour heaven and hell before they return to earth. The play mixed farce and religious piety. Nagle and Healey considered *The Black Sheep of Heaven* and *The Bums of Heaven*, before settling on the English title, *Hoboes in Heaven*. The production ran for four weeks but did not get a favorable press.

For the next production Father Nagle chose a play that had been produced by the Los Angeles Catholic Theatre Conference and that had gained extensive media coverage. The play was *Trial by Fire*, a docu-drama by Father George H. Dunne, S. J. Dunne based his play on the tragic case of the Shorts, a black family of four who moved into a "restricted" area in Fontana, San Bernadino County, Calfornia.[34] On Christmas Day 1945, their home exploded and all four members of the family were killed. Despite testimony about kerosene-soaked ground around the house, the coroner's jury ruled that the explosion was accidental. Father Dunne was teaching political science at the time at Loyola University of Los Angeles. A former missionary in China with a Ph.D. in international relations from the University of Chicago, Dunne had become involved in the struggle for racial justice while teaching at Saint Louis University. Enraged at what happened in San Bernadino, he wrote a series of articles about the case in Catholic publications and lectured before Catholic audiences. Neither produced the results he hoped for. A nun friend of his suggested that he write a play based on the facts of the case. Never having written a play before, Dunne decided to use a documentary approach and he took more than half the dialogue in the play verbatim from the inquest stenographer's notes. He also interviewed friends and relatives of the Short family as well as court and law enforcement officers. The play employed two stages, which alternately "blacked out." On one the coroner's investigation proceeded; on the other appeared flashbacks of the actual events before the explosion. Dunne had the lawyers in the trial address the audience directly and the "coroner's jury" sat in the front row of the theatre. The Los Angeles production was very successful, despite attacks calling Dunne "a tool of the Communists subverting the American way of life." Dunne spoke after the opening of the play and urged the audience to vote in favor of an anti-restrictive covenant law then before the California legislature. *Ebony* magazine did a feature story on the production and praised Father Dunne's courage.

Nagle was enthusiastic about the play but wasn't sure how it would fare in New York where the explosion and trial had received less notice and interest. Father Nagle asked Albert McCleery, who had been stage manager for Guthrie McClintic and who was then director of theatre at Fordham University, to direct. William Riva, who had worked with McCleery for eight years, designed the sets. Nappy Whiting, a member of the Los Angeles cast, came to New York at his own expense to audition for the Blackfriars production. Whiting had played a variety of small parts in films, mainly servants. He considered the play his special mission.[35] During performances of the play, members of the Social Workers Party passed out pamphlets entitled "Vigilante Terror in Fontana" in front of the theatre. The pamphlet carried a photograph of the Los Angeles cast of *Trial by Fire*.[36] It was not the kind of support Father Nagle wanted. Father Dunne had already been accused of being a communist sympathizer and Nagle did not want conservative Catholics to think that Blackfriars had anything in common with the Socialist Workers Party. However, he made no effort to stop the pamphlets.

The *Daily Mirror* called *Trial by Fire* "a dramatic and eloquent plea for racial understanding."[37] The *Post* termed the play "an earnest and sincere piece of writing . . . and the kind of play a non-commercial group should produce. Its message is one that should be repeated time and time again."[38] *Women's Wear Daily* stated, "Though graphic and frequently gripping, it never overstates its case. Although moving, it is never overwrought and is, therefore, always convincing. Father Dunne has discharged an important service to the theatre of propaganda."[39] The *Wall Street Journal* called the play "a dramatic story that is smoothly told, beautifully staged and perfectly enacted."[40] *Billboard* called it "a timely and often moving plea for social justice" and said that "all in all, the Blackfriars are to be heartily commended for a sincere and significant effort."[41] The *Morning Telegraph* said, "Despite its inadequacies as a play, it is well worth seeing. Congratulations to Father Dunne and Albert McCleery."[42]

Actor's Cue, a professional publication for actors, said,

> It's about time our theatre began throwing some posies at the Blackfriars for their yeoman work the past five years and particularly their fine efforts in the battle against racial discrimination.
>
> Aside from the magnificent production which they now have running in their 200 seat theatre, the conscientious attitude of the little Blackfriars troupe of managers and directors toward the theatre and society's problems deserves some special commendation from theatrical folk. *Actor's Cue* urges you to see it. . . . We throw our hats in the air to Blackfriars, Father Dunne and Albert McCleery.[43]

The *Peoples Voice*, a black newspaper in New York, said, "It is a moving drama which should be seen by everyone, not only for the message it holds but also for its technical perfection."[44] Another black publication, the *Louisville Defender*, called the play "stirring and dynamic" and pointed out that Father Dunne "has been attacked by powerful real estate interests and men of his own faith. . . . This experimental group shows considerable courage in bringing *Trial by Fire* to the New York public."[45]

Despite the support from the Socialist Workers, Blackfriars was very pleased with the production of *Trial by Fire*. It had been an artistic success and its message was something the theatre group believed in deeply, the kind of play that made their Catholic theatre venture worthwhile. Father Nagle recalled the reaction of Nappy Whiting to the experience of being in the production:

> At the cast party he made a little speech, and it was only then that I realized the extent of his sacrifice and degree of devotion to the cause. . . . Beginning by telling us that he just wandered into the Los Angeles production and sort of got caught in it, he went on to say that it began to mean something to him. Then he heard of the Blackfriars production and thought he ought to get re-established in the cast. . . . It was only later that he realized we didn't pay any salaries. Nappy didn't mind that too much, but he wasn't sure how he was going to manage in New York--having been away for a good many years. . . . That night at the cast party, instead of blaming us, he paid tribute to Blackfriars for taking up his cause--Blackfriars and the Church.[46]

While *Trial by Fire* was still running, Merritt Wyatt told Nagle that he was retiring because of failing eyesight and general poor health.

Wyatt, husband of drama critic Euphemia Van Rensselaar Wyatt and father of actress Jane Wyatt, had been financial and box office manager for the theatre for seven years and for the first four years received no salary at all. Carey found a woman to replace him and the woman's husband also occasionally helped out in the office.[47]

At about the same time Father Reilly, an old friend of Nagle's from the Blackfriars' summer theatre at Nabnasset, Massachusetts, paid him a visit. In the course of the conversation, Reilly asked Nagle if he had ever thought of writing a play about Our Lady of Fatima.[48] Nagle liked the idea and, since he needed an explicitly religious play for the Lenten season, spent the Christmas holidays writing *Lady of Fatima*. The play treated the apparitions of the Virgin Mary to three shepherd children near the village of Fatima, Portugal in 1917. The message of the Virgin to the children was the necessity of repentance and praying for world peace. The negative reactions of religious skeptics and the efforts of the anti-religious socialist government then in power to silence the children provided the conflict.

In early January, before the script was even finished, Nagle issued press releases to the *New York Times*, the *Journal-American*, the *Catholic News* and the *Brooklyn Tablet* announcing auditions for children to play the young shepherds. He also sent announcements to all the parochial schools in the area. Two hundred and thirty children showed up for the auditions.[49] One of the three children cast was sixth grader Edward Villela from Bayside, Long Island.[50] Young Villela had appeared in several shows staged by the Young Artists Group and was studying ballet at the School of the American Ballet Theatre.

Nagle's final script, which was barely finished in time for rehearsals, called for a cast of thirty-five actors and for twelve sets. Designer David Reppa solved the problem of multiple scene changes by designing a unit set. Nagle and Carey went into production with caution and fear. The play had been hastily written and the physical requirements of the play stretched Blackfriars' small stage to the limit.

While not the critical success that *Trial by Fire* was, *Lady of Fatima* received a favorable press. Lester Bernstein of the *Times* wrote:

> As the play's sponsors acknowledge, its appeal is limited by its dogmatic approach to a religious subject, the appearance of miraculous apparitions to three children in Fatima, Portugal in 1917. Within this

limitation, however, it has the benefit of some effective writing and a job of direction by Dennis Gurney, that draw sincere performances from the young children at the hub of the story. Its sectarian appeal should be strong.[51]

Robert Coleman wrote in the *Daily Mirror* that "it tells an inspiring story dramatically. It held the interest of the first-nighters throughout."[52] The critics gave their highest praise to the three young actors who played the children.[53] George Freedley of the *Morning Telegraph* stated: "Anna Stubits as Lucia, Naomi Mitty as tiny Jacinta and Edward Villela as Francisco are really superior actors and should go far in the theatre. They are completely natural and fresh. . . . Frankly, they are the best reason I can think of for attending *Lady of Fatima.*[54]

The play was so popular with Catholic audiences that it was completely sold out for its six week run and had to be re-opened after Easter for an additional three weeks. Even before the production closed, Nagle received requests from amateur Catholic groups who wanted to produce the play. Nagle sold the amateur rights to the Declan McMullen Company of New York who published the play.[55]

Near the end of the run of *Lady of Fatima* and after Nagle had negotiated with the McMullen Company, he was approached by two Irishmen living in New York, William and Paul Henebery. The Heneberys asked Nagle if they could have the professional rights to *Lady of Fatima* for Ireland and Scotland.[56] They told Nagle they were interested in spreading devotion to the Virgin Mary, that they had theatrical connections in Ireland and Scotland, but had very little money. Nagle agreed to give them the professional rights for Ireland and Scotland for one year. All he asked in return was ten percent of the net profits for Blackfriars and their agreement to hire Dennis Gurney as their director. Gurney hadn't seen his mother in England for twenty-eight years and Nagle thought this would be a good way to get Gurney a free trip to England. When the contract was drawn up, it read to include "professional rights worldwide" because the two men said that if the production was successful in Ireland, they might take the play to Australia.[57] Nagle agreed, but didn't notice that the contract also mentioned "a share in the motion picture, amateur, radio and television rights."

The Heneberys never produced *Lady of Fatima* in Ireland and

Gurney didn't get a trip home to England. Instead the two brothers, calling themselves "Fatima Productions," began a New York production through Equity Theatre Library using unsalaried actors. Trouble occurred when the Veronica Players, an amateur group in Union City, New Jersey, announced their production of *Lady of Fatima*, licensed through Declan McMullen. Heneberys' attorney wrote to the Veronica Players and demanded that they either cease production or pay a percentage of the gross profits to them. Letters went back and forth between attorneys about whether the Equity Theatre Library production was "professional," whether Nagle intended to grant the Heneberys amateur rights, the rights of the Declan McMullen Company, etc. until the summer of 1949. The Heneberys' production was a complete failure, the term of the contract--whatever its conditions--expired, and the matter died. However, Fr. Nagle's lack of care in financial matters would later come back to haunt him.

For the fall of 1948 Blackfriars acquired a script that centered on the life and songs of Tom Moore, an Irish singer and composer of ballads and one of the leaders of the Irish rebellion of 1798. The play, *The Minstrel Boy*, had been written by W. A. Douglas, a newspaperman, several years before but was never produced. For a while actor Frank Fay held an option on it. The play included songs such as "Believe Me If All Those Endearing Young Charms," "The Harp That Once Through Tara's Hall," and "The Ministrel Boy." The script called for three actors to play the part of Moore--one as a boy, one as a young man and another as an old man. Blackfriars advertised its search for the three actors who also had to be tenor singers. The critics generally agreed that the play itself was poor but that the renditions of the songs were beautiful.

Father Nagle had wanted to write a play about Blessed Martin de Porres for quite some time. The Dominicans had long fostered devotion to Blessed Martin as the patron of racial justice and were eager for his canonization as a saint. Martin de Porres (1579-1639) was the illegitimate son of a Spanish nobleman and a black woman in Lima, Peru. Inheriting his mother's dark color, he experienced racial discrimination early in his life. Never embittered, he was characterized by his gentleness and affability. A physician befriended him at the age of twelve and taught him the art of healing. In his late teens he entered the Dominican Priory of the Holy Rosary in Lima as a lay brother. He served as the infirmarian of the priory, but even in religious life he encountered racial prejudice. However, he soon became an example of sanctity to the other friars because of his visions, ecstasies, austere penances and long nights in prayer. Many said he performed miraculous cures, sometimes even by a mere touch, and that he had astonishing communication with animals. He was admired for his kindness to all, his humility and his generosity to the poor. Many, including nobles and high ranking churchmen, sought him out for spiritual advice. The church finally canonized him a saint in 1962.

Since the process of Blessed Martin's canonization was in progress, Nagle visited Father Norbert Georges, O.P., the Dominican priest who headed the Blessed Martin Guild and served as one of the official promoters of the cause for his canonization. Father Georges allowed Nagle to examine the eight hundred pages of the official text of the proposal for Martin's canonization. This included testimonies from contemporaries of Martin given before an ecclesiastical court.[58] These records became the basis for *City of Kings*. The first act of the play dealt with Martin's childhood and the second and third acts with his life in the Dominican priory.

Since casting would be difficult for the production, especially for the role of Martin, Blackfriars issued a call for African-American actors and specifically contacted black publications like the *Pittsburgh Courier*.[59] Nagle and Gurney finally cast Elwood Smith as Martin. Smith had attended Xavier University in New Orleans and had a music degree from Julliard. Though he made his living mainly as a night club singer, Smith had played leading roles with the American Negro Theatre. The cast also included Anthony Franciosa as Brother Bernardo, a Dominican novice who at first made racial slurs about Martin.[60]

City of the Kings proved to be a hit. Williams Hawkins of the *World Telegram* called the play "an unusual work presented with a rare combination of reverence and humor."[61] Whitney Bolton of the *Morning Telegraph* wrote, "I went to *City of Kings* as a stranger. I came away warmed, pleased and happy. . . . Few performances in the current theatre in New York match the work of Elwood Smith."[62] Thomas Dash said in *Women's Wear Daily*, "It is interesting and instructive and focuses its spotlight on a truly beatific character. . . .

Rev. Nagle contributes a great deal toward inter-racial amity with the
little known biography of this colored saint."[63] Dash also had praise
for the acting of Smith. Bob Francis of *Billboard* stated, "It is a
pleasure to report that Father Urban Nagle's latest effort . . . is a
decidedly timely and thoughtful document in these days of intolerant
stress. . . . Elwood Smith gives a splendid account of himself as
Martin. . . . There is quiet humor and humanity in the reading."[64]
Robert Coleman of the *Daily Mirror* said that "the cast is one of the
best yet assembled at Blackfriars," and called the play "a moving and
absorbing study of a great soul."[65] Coleman referred to Smith's
performance as "touching and sensitive." Jack Shanley of the *Times*
said the play was "a rich and compelling story" and "refreshing
theatre," and added that "Smith plays the role of the zealous Martin
with moving intensity."[66] Richard Watts of the *Post* wrote,

> One of the most difficult things conceivable on the rebellious stage is to
> present a picture of holiness. Almost inevitably the result is unbearable
> smugness and painful mawkishness. Thanks to Father Nagle's skill and,
> in particular, to the inescapably winning performance in the leading role
> of a young Negro actor named Elwood Smith, these pitfalls are
> completely eluded and *City of Kings* emerges from its dangers as a warm,
> touching and entirely believable portrait of a saintly and selfless man.
>
> It is meant for the edification of believers. But Blessed Martin, as author
> and actor present him, is an appealing figure, without reference to
> theology, and the play has a quiet appeal that is not far from
> irresistible.[67]

T. A. Wise of the *Wall Street Journal* thought the play was
"skillfully written with a fine blending of bitterness, love, religion and
humor."[68] Wise too had high praise for the lead, "Elwood Smith gives
a superb portrayal of the tolerant and zealous Martin." The reviewer
for *Variety* termed the play "a notable achievement" which "holds the
attention throughout. Elwood Smith," *Variety* continued, "gives a
moving and sensitive portrayal of the central character." [69]
Once again, a critic for the *Pittsburgh Courier* reviewed a
Blackfriars production. He called *City of Kings* "brilliant" and said
"the drama has wit, pathos, excitement and perception far beyond the
usual Broadway production."[70]
City of Kings was the fourth play Blackfriars had done using

African-American actors. In the early 1960's, writing to a friend, Nagle commented about the place of the black in the American theatre. Nagle wrote that "he [the black] will not get equality in the theatre until he gets it in life." He stated further, "I do not want the Negro actor to be limited to his (or her) traditional role as maid, cook, chauffeur, delivery boy." But Nagle recalled facing the problem of blacks in stereotyped roles in the casting of *Caukey*:

> The Negroes had to be the Ivy Leaguers, the articulate, the smooth. I encountered some good actors, known in the profession (some with good scholastic backgrounds) and they couldn't make the switch.

> One of them told me that he made his living being what audiences expected a Negro to be and do. He said that thirty or so years as a Negro entertainer (although he was a good actor) made it too difficult to maintain a role without some slips. He had accepted his fate and didn't care to make the effort for a role which would never come again.

Nagle also remembered the bitterness of one black actor in the cast of *City of Kings*:

> One of the Negroes was belligerently anti-white and showed it to the point of saying at the cast party on closing night, "Unless I was the best actor you could find for the part, you wouldn't have me around here for five minutes." And he was right. But not because he was a Negro. It was simply because he fought the cast--black and white. I was happy to learn that whites behaved quite well but that could be because of their greater security. [71]

A trial in New York in the summer of 1949 of eleven communists on espionage charges provided the basis for the play that opened the 1949-50 season. The trial got wide publicity all over the country, but especially in New York. Father Nagle, who had strong feelings about communist infiltration in the United States, thought it might be appropriate for Blackfriars to stage an anti-communist play. Perhaps he also thought it might be advantageous to answer conservative critics who had hinted at Blackfriars' leftist leanings because of the theatre's production of four plays about racial prejudice in five years.

The idea became a docu-drama entitled *Shake Hands With the Devil*, written by Nagle and his former student, Robert Healey, although only Healey's name appeared on the script and in the publicity.[72] The play consisted of six episodes based on six actual events which showed communist treachery. The six episodes were placed within the frame story of a trial of communist spies.

Some theatre people reacted negatively to such a blatantly anti-communist play. Senator Joseph McCarthy was just beginning his infamous investigations into Communist infiltration and film, television and theatre were a particular target. Forty-two actors and technicians walked out of the production between the time they got their final assignments and opening night. Besides the walk-out of some actors and technicians, another problem presented itself. A spokesman for the United States Justice Department came to Nagle and said he thought the play shouldn't open until the trial of the eleven communists closed, lest it should be used in the expected appeal as a prejudicial incident. The spokesman said that Blackfriars might use the episodes of communist activity, but asked that the production not contain direct references to or quotes from the trial. Consequently Nagle and Healey prepared a different frame for the episodes, but the trial closed a few days before the play opened. The actors who remained in the cast were frightened of possible retaliation so Nagle arranged to have police agents in the audience during the performance opening night.

Despite the play's lack of subtlety, the production received a generally favorable press. The *Wall Street Journal* called *Shake Hands with the Devil* "a work that has brought forth a combination of speed, imagination and timeliness."[73] *Billboard's* critic wrote that "it carries a ring of truth and is completely interesting thruout. . . . Healey and the Blackfriars are to be congratulated for their outspokenness."[74]

In the group's spring production, *Armor of Light* by Father Nagle, he attempted to chronicle all of the missionary travels of Saint Paul. Consequently the play required a cast of fifty-two with twenty-four scenes. Most critics pointed out the rambling quality of the production and Richard Watts of the *Post* compared the play unfavorably to Nagle's earlier efforts, *Savonarola* and *City of Kings*.[75] The play was popular with the Catholic audiences and the run had to be extended for an additional three weeks. The production also got a favorable mention in *Cue* magazine for actress Geraldine Page, who played Mersina, "a disreputable woman" who heckles Saint Paul while he preaches.[76] "I got lots of laughs being very irreverant to

Saint Paul," she said. Page recalled that the cast was so large that for years afterward "I was always running into people who were in *Armor of Light*."[77]

Shortly after *Armor of Light* closed Nagle received a notice from the directors of the School of Radio Technique, which leased the building and sublet the auditorium to Blackfriars, that they would be taking possession of the theatre on November 1 and that Blackfriars' sublease would not be renewed for the coming year.[78] Nagle and Carey spent most of the summer looking for a new theatre, but could find nothing that they could afford. They had nearly given up hope of being able to open their fall production, when early in the fall, Franklin Hauser of the School of Radio Technique came into Blackfriars' office. In conversation he revealed to Nagle that the owners had offered him and his partner, John Gilbert, the auditorium for three times what Blackfriars was paying. Assuming that Blackfriars had decided to move elsewhere, Franklin and Gilbert decided to rent the space even though they weren't exactly sure yet what they would do with it. Franklin assured Nagle that they would not occupy the theatre as long as Blackfriars wanted it. Franklin invited Blackfriars to play a full schedule of productions in the theatre at the old rent in exchange for occasional use by the School of Radio Technique for classes and productions. Nagle and Franklin also discussed the possibility of Blackfriars becoming involved in television programming.

During the desperate search for a theatre, Nagle received a letter from Father Terence S. McDermott, O.P., his provincial superior. McDermott said he was distressed to learn of the loss of the theatre and added "I am keenly interested in this activity. . . ."[79] He continued, "It is my wish that you continue producing plays under the auspices of Blackfriars. It is also my wish that you confine your activities to Blackfriars." It is apparent from this letter that Nagle had the support of his provincial superior but also that McDermott was not happy with Nagle's other activities and consequent absences from Blackfriars.

Because of the persistent difficulty of getting scripts and also because of internal problems, Blackfriars again produced only two plays for the 1950-51 season.

The first production, *Angel With Red Hair* by Ted Farrah, a Canadian newspaperman with the Associated Press, was a comedy-fantasy about a young woman who saves a chapel in Quebec from destruction at the hands of greedy real estate promoters. She is assisted in her effort by the spirit of Brother Hilaire who, although he has been dead for two hundred years, watches over the fortunes of the villagers. Brother Hilaire, who never appears, merely laughs robustly at the final curtain. Dennis Gurney got his friend, actor Edward Arnold, to make a recording of his laugh which was used in the production.[80] Robert Coleman summed up the critical response when he called the play "a pleasant little comedy."[81]

In the spring Blackfriars made its first attempt at producing an opera. Nagle received a libretto and score called *Open the Gates*, an opera about the life of Christ, but as seen from the perspective of Mary Magdalene. The libretto was by Robert Payne and the music by Dai-Keong-Lee. Dai-Keong Lee was an Hawaiian born Chinese-American who had studied at the Julliard School of Music. In 1950 he had premiered a symphony at Carnegie Hall, and had conducted orchestras in the United States, Canada, Australia and the Philippines. Lee later composed the music for the original Broadway production of *The Teahouse of the August Moon*. Payne was the British-born author of fifteen books who had been a war correspondent in China. The reaction of the critics was mixed. The *Times* said: "Mr. Lee's music is grave and respectful. He can write a melodic line of sustained length. . . ."[82] But the *New Yorker* said of the opera: "To be at all moving, it would have to be invested with exalted music and Mr. Lee's score, alas, comes nowhere near the mark, sounding neither devout nor passionate."[83]

In the spring of 1951, Warner Brothers Pictures, Inc. expressed interest in filming Nagle's *Lady of Fatima*. Warner Brothers later decided, however, that since the story of Fatima was in the public domain, it would be more advantageous for them to have their own writers prepare an original screenplay. This resulted in *Miracle of Our Lady of Fatima*, starring Gilbert Roland and Angela Clark, which Warner Brothers released in 1952. They did ask Nagle to serve as technical advisor to the production since he was both a priest and well versed on the incidents at Fatima. In July 1951, Nagle signed a contract with Warner Brothers to serve as adviser to the motion picture for a salary of $150.00 a week, a sum Father Carey thought ridiculously low.[84] Father McDermott gave his permission. However, McDermott later received a letter from Francis Cardinal McIntyre, archbishop of Los Angeles where the motion picture was being filmed.[85] McIntyre did not object to Nagle's work in the film, but did object to the use of Nagle's name since the Church had no right of approval on the screenplay and might be embarrassed by its content. As an addendum, he also mentioned that he felt Warner Brothers was taking advantage of Nagle by using his expertise for only $150.00 a week. Consequently, Nagle served as adviser to the film, but his name never appeared in the credits.

While *Open the Gates* had been playing, another drama developed behind the scenes. The relationship between Father Nagle and Father Carey was quickly deteriorating.[86] The conflict had multiple aspects. Carey objected to Nagle's numerous other activities--radio, television, books and lectures---and his frequent absences from the theatre. He felt that Nagle had no business ability and had made some bad deals, especially in regard to the professional rights for *Lady of Fatima*. Likewise he disapproved of the agreement that Nagle had made with the School of Radio Technique and the possible involvement of Blackfriars in television. Carey thought that Blackfriars should have used the threatened eviction from the building as an opportunity to start a fund-raising campaign to build its own theatre, an idea that Nagle thought impractical. Carey also disagreed with the way money was being managed at Blackfriars and he thought that Nagle placed too much trust in the woman who managed the theatre's financial affairs, a woman who had been hired by Carey. And though the two priests had gotten along well for years, one cannot overlook the basic differences in their personalities. Nagle was creative, affable and outgoing and was known for his humor and storytelling ability. Carey was organized, reserved, insular and conservative. It is not impossible that jealousy played a part in the controversy.

Carey had threatened to resign from Blackfriars in July 1950. However, in February 1951, a few days before *Open the Gates* premiered, Carey wrote a letter to Father McDermott accusing the office-financial manager of stealing money. In addition, Carey set forth his other grievances against Nagle. In regards to finances he said: "You should see some of the agreements Fr. Nagle has signed--without my knowledge--with phonies and broken-down publishers, which have cost the Order plenty." In regards to Nagle's other activities he wrote: "For 20 years Nagle has yapped about a Catholic theatre. . . . To hell with radio, television, lectures and other books."[87]

Nagle supported his financial manager and eventually the woman and her husband hired an attorney. The controversy dragged on through the summer and became more and more bitter. There were letters from Carey to McDermott, Nagle to McDermott, various lay people to McDermott, and letters from attorneys to everyone. At the end of August or early in September, Father McDermott wrote to an involved third party and said, "It is my intention to appoint Father Nagle as legal head of Blackfriars . . . and have Father Carey separate himself from Blackfriars."[88] McDermott also stated in the letter that he had informed Nagle of the fact before Nagle left for California on business. However, on September 19, 1951, McDermott sent letters to both Nagle and Carey, reversing that decision. He wrote to Nagle that "for reasons of health, I am removing you as Director of the Blackfriars Guild."[89] He appointed Carey as director of Blackfriars, "effective immediately."[90] In January, 1952 McDermott assigned Nagle as chaplain at the Dominican Sisters' Motherhouse of Saint Mary of the Springs in Columbus, Ohio. Later an independent audit of Blackfriars records revealed no financial irregularities.

The reason why the provincial, Father McDermott, transferred Father Nagle is unclear. Perhaps he believed Father Carey's accusations about mismanagement. There were rumors about Nagle's excessive drinking. Nagle, in fact, liked nothing better then to have a few drinks and then regale his listeners with humorous stories. The butt of his jokes was sometimes Father McDermott. McDermott had been re-elected to several terms as provincial (regional superior) by building himself the ecclesiastical equivalent of a political machine. He and his colleagues were fodder for Nagle's sardonic wit and some of the barbs must certainly have gotten back to McDermott. The talent that allowed Nagle to write comedies may also have been his undoing.

A more probable explanation, however, is that Carey's vision of Blackfriars was more in keeping with McDermott's. Nagle had always seen Blackfriars as an authentic Dominican ministry in itself and was only concerned with breaking even financially. Carey, a more practical than an aesthetic man, looked upon the theatre as a way of preaching the gospel, but in addition he viewed it as a possible instrument for making money to support the Order's other works. Carey very likely presented this view to McDermott, who was more likely to approve of his approach. In fact, in subsequent years Blackfriars made regular and substantial financial contributions to St. Joseph's Province for its "real" apostolic works, such as parishes and schools.

Nagle served as chaplain to the Dominican Sisters until his death and also taught part-time at the College of Saint Mary of the Springs, a small liberal arts college for women on the same campus. He continued being active in the National Catholic Theatre Conference and in radio and television, writing for *The Catholic Hour*.

Father Urban Voll, O.P., who lived with Father Nagle at Saint Mary of the Springs from 1956 to 1960, remembers him as a delightful companion to live with who kept the other priests assigned there entertained at the dinner table with his stories and comments.[91] Voll stated that Nagle seldom spoke about the Blackfriars and then only in the most general terms. He added that he never heard Nagle make a single derogatory remark about Father Carey. Father Voll, who was the religious superior, does remember having to correct Father Nagle once about his excessive drinking, even though Nagle "was very funny when he had been drinking." At the end of the reprimand, he asked Nagle about the money he used to buy liquor since money was very tight for the priests and every penny had to be accounted for with the provincial office back in New York. Nagle smiled and said, "I write it down as entertainment." "Well, stop it," responded Voll, "I'm not entertained."

Though various projects and vacations brought Father Nagle back to New York occasionally, he never entered the Blackfriars Theatre again. When he died from a heart ailment in 1965, at the age of 59, the General Assembly of Rhode Island, the state of his birth, issued an expression of sympathy to the Dominican Order.

Because of the long and bitter controversy, the need to completely reorganize the staff and the lack of a script, Blackfriars did not produce a play in the fall of 1951. It was the first time in ten years that Blackfriars had not opened a fall production.

1. All information on performances, ticket prices, fund-raising and promotion is taken from various mimeographed sheets in the Blackfriars Collection, Providence College Archives, Providence, R.I.

2. Urban Nagle, O.P., to Clarence Derwent, n.d. (sometime in 1948), Nagle papers, Dominican Archives, Washington, D.C.

3. Ibid.

4. Information on scene designers is based on various play programs, Black-friars Collection.

5. The books mentioned are *Uncle George and Uncle Malachy* (Milwaukee: Bruce Publishing Company, 1946) and *Behind the Masque* (New York: McMullen Books, 1951).

6. Urban Nagle, O.P., to Henry C. Graham, O.P., n.d. (sometime in 1945), Nagle papers.

7. T.S. McDermott, O.P., to Urban Nagle, O.P., 18 October 1945, Nagle papers.

8. Otis L. Guernsey, Jr., "Seven Mirrors," *New York Herald-Tribune*, 26 October 1945.

9. Geraldine Page later appeared in *Armor of Light* at Blackfriars. Since then she appeared in almost two dozen productions on and off Broadway, including *Summer and Smoke, The Rainmaker, Sweet Bird of Youth, The Three Sisters* and *Agnes of God*. Her many films include *Hondo, Summer and Smoke, Sweet Bird of Youth, Toys in the Attic , Day of the Locust* and *The Pope of Greenwich Village*. She won NATAS (Emmy) Awards for her performances in *A Christmas Memory* and *The Thanksgiving Visitor*, and was nominated for an Academy Award three times. Page won the Academy Award for best actress in 1985 for *A Trip to Bountiful*. She died in 1987.

Patricia Neal made her Broadway debut in *Another Part of the Forest* and later appeared in *The Children's Hour, Roomful of Roses, Suddenly, Last Summer* and *The Miracle Worker*. She has appeared in many films, most notably *The Fountainhead, The Hasty Heart, A Face in the Crowd, Breakfast at Tiffany's, Hud, In Harm's Way*, and *The Subject Was Roses*. She won an Antoinette Perry (Tony) Award for her performance in *Another Part of the Forest* and an Academy Award for *Hud*.

10. Robert Coleman, "The Theatre," *New York Daily Mirror*, 26 October 1945.

11. Louis Peterson, Jr. later became a successful playwright and screen writer. His plays, *Take a Giant Step* and *Entertain a Ghost*, were produced on Broadway and he wrote the screenplays for *The Tempest* and *Take a Giant Step*. Peterson was nominated for an NATAS (Emmy) Award for his television play, *Joey*.

12. Edba, "A Young American," *Variety*, 30 January 1946.

13. Robert Coleman, "The Theatre," *New York Daily Mirror*, 19 January 1946.

14. Robert Casey, "A Plus for This One," *Chicago News*, 27 February 1946.

15. Claudia Cassidy, "On the Aisle," *Chicago Tribune*, 27 February 1946.

16. Urban Nagle, O.P., *Behind the Masque* (New York: McMullen Company, 1951), 242.

17. Robert Anderson later wrote *Tea and Sympathy, All Summer Long, Silent Night/Lonely Night, You Know I Can't Hear You When The Water's Running* (in which another Blackfriars veteran, Eileen Heckart, appeared), and *I Never Sang for My Father*. He wrote the screenplays for *Tea and Sympathy, Until They Sail, The Nun's Story, The Sand Pebbles, Night of the Generals* and *I Never Sang for My Father*. He was nominated for an Academy Award for *The Nun's Story*. Anderson has also written for radio and television.

18. George Freedley, "The Stage Today," *New York Morning Telegraph*, 21 May 1946.

19. Kelsey Allen, "Come Marching Home," *Women's Wear Daily*, 20 May 1946

20. Robert Coleman, "The Theatre," *New York Daily Mirror*, 20 May 1946.

21. Edba, "Come Marching Home," *Variety*, 20 May 1946.

22. Otis L. Guernsey, Jr., "Come Marching Home," *New York Herald-Tribune*, 20 May 1946.

23. Judy Shepard, "Snow Shovels and Cocktails Fail Him," *New York Post*, 24 July 1946.

24. Ralph Land, "Theatre With a Purpose," *Christian Family*, February 1955, 3.

25. All financial information in this section is taken from carbon copies of typewritten sheets in the Blackfriars Collection.

26. King Donovan later became a supporting actor in films and television. He was also the husband and manager of comedienne, Imogene Coca.

27. "Off-Broadway Openings," *Billboard*, 1 November 1946.

28. Urban Nagle, O.P., to Clarence Derwent, n.d. (sometime in 1948), Nagle papers.

29. Darren McGavin came to national attention in 1949 when he replaced Cameron Mitchell in the role of Happy in *Death of a Salesman*. Among other plays, he appeared in *My Three Angels, The Rainmaker* (opposite Geraldine Page), *Tunnel of Love* and *Blood, Sweat and Stanley Poole*. He also appeared in such films as *The Court Martial of Billy Mitchell* and *The Man With the Golden Arm*. However, McGavin is best known for the five television series in which he appeared, especially *Mike Hammer*. Most recently McGavin has appeared in the role of Murphy's father on the television comedy series, "Murphy Brown."

30. William Hawkins, "The Theatre," *New York World-Telegram*, 7 March 1947.

31. Program, *Respectfully Yours* by Peggy Lamson, 13 May - 28 May 1947, Blackfriars Collection.

32. Robert Coleman, "The Theatre," *New York Daily Mirror*, 29 October 1947.

33. Nagle, *Behind the Masque*, 261.

34. All information about the Short family and the Los Angeles production of *Trial by Fire* is from: "*Trial by Fire* Stirs Audience to Boos and Tears," *Ebony*, June 1947, 104-110.

35. Nagle, *Behind the Masque*, 270.

36. Ibid., 269.

37. Robert Coleman, The Theatre," *New York Daily Mirror*, 5 December 1947.

38. Vernon Rice, "Theatre," *New York Post*, 5 December 1947.

39. Thomas R. Dash, "Trial by Fire," *Women's Wear Daily*, 8 December 1947.

40. T.A.W., "The Theatre," *Wall Street Journal*, 11 December 1947.

41. Bob Francis, "Trial by Fire," *Billboard*, 12 December 1947.

42. George Freedley, "The Stage Today," *New York Morning Telegraph*, 6 December 1947.

43. "City Desk on Broadway," *Actor's Cue*, December 1947, 2.

44. "*Trial by Fire* at Blackfriars," *People's Voice*, 13 December 1947.

45. "*Trial by Fire* Attacks Restrictive Covenants," *Louisville Defender*, 14 December 1947.

46. Nagle, *Behind the Masque*, 270-271.

47. Ibid., 279.

48. Ibid., 272.

49. "Chosen for Blackfriars Role," *Brooklyn Tablet*, 31 January 1948.

50. In 1957 Edward Villela joined the New York City Ballet and eventually became a soloist and principal dancer and one of America's top ballet stars. He created many roles in George Balanchine's ballets, the most famous of which was *The Prodigal Son*. Villela also starred in the musical *Brigadoon* in 1962 and he was the subject of an NBC television film, *A Man Who Dances* in 1968. He is presently choreographer for the New York City Ballet.

51. Lester Bernstein, "Lenten Play Presented," *New York Times*, 13 February 1948.

52. Robert Coleman, "The Theatre," *New York Daily Mirror*, 13 February 1948.

53. Edba, "Lady of Fatima," *Variety*, 18 February 1948.

54. George Freedley, "The Stage Today," *New York Morning Telegraph*, 14 February 1948.

55. Between 1948 and 1951 *Lady of Fatima* had 556 amateur performances.

56. Information in this section is based on the following letters in the Nagle

papers: Paul P. Henebery and William J. Henebery to Urban Nagle, O.P., 15 September 1948; Urban Nagle, O.P. to Paul D. O'Brien, attorney, 20 September 1948; Urban Nagle, O.P. to Declan McMullen Company, 29 September 1948; Amos S. Basel, attorney to Father Benjamin, P.C. (Union City, N.J.), 24 September 1948; John R. Kelly (Union City, N.J.) to Amos S. Basel, attorney, 6 October 1958; Paul D. O'Brien to Amos S. Basel, 7 March and 16 June 1949.

57. Contract between Urban Nagle, O.P. and Paul P. and William J. Henebery, 24 March 1958, Nagle papers.

58. Nagle, *Behind the Masque*, 287.

59. "*City of Kings* Issues Call for Sepia Actors," *Pittsburgh Courier*, 4 December 1948.

60. Anthony Franciosa appeared in over two dozen films, among them: *A Face in the Crowd, Wild is the Wind, A Hatful of Rain, The Long Hot Summer, Period of Adjustment* and *The Pleasure Seekers*. He has also appeared in many television productions.

61. William Hawkins, "The Theatre," *New York World-Telegram*, 27 February 1949.

62. Whitney Bolton, "The Stage," *New York Morning Telegraph*, 18 February 1949.

63. Thomas R. Dash, "City of Kings," *Women's Wear Daily*, 23 February 1949.

64. Bob Francis, "City of Kings," *Billboard*, 26 February 1949.

65. Robert Coleman, "The Theatre," *New York Daily Mirror*, 18 February 1949.

66. Jack P. Shanley, "City of Kings," *New York Times*, 18 February 1949.

67. Richard Watts, Jr., "Theatre," *New York Post*, 18 February 1949.

68. T.A.W., "Theatre," *Wall Street Journal*, 21 February 1949.

69. Edba, "City of Kings," *Variety*, 23 February 1949.

70. G.S.S., "City of Kings," *Pittsburgh Courier*, 25 February 1949.

71. Urban Nagle, O.P., Letter to "Don," n.d. (sometime in the early 1960's), Nagle papers.

72. All information about the writing and production of *Shake Hands With the Devil* is from Nagle, *Behind the Masque*, 294-298.

73. T.A.W., "Theatre," *Wall Street Journal*, 22 October 1949.

74. Bob Francis, "Off-Broadway Reviews," *Billboard*, 29 October 1949.

75. Richard Watts, "Two on the Aisle," *New york Post*, 24 February 1950.

76. Gilbert W. Gabriel, "New Play on B'way," *Cue*, 4 March 1950.

77. Geraldine Page, interview with the author, 20 October 1982.

78. Bob Francis, "Off-Broadway Reviews," *Billboard*, 29 October 1949.

79. T.S. McDermott, O.P., to Urban Nagle, O.P., 12 October 1950, Nagle papers.

80. Nagle, *Behind the Masque*, 303.

81. Robert Coleman, "The Theatre," *New York Daily Mirror*, 25 October 1950.

82. H.T., "Blackfriars Offer Premier of Opera," *New York Times*, 23 February 1951.

83. Douglas Watt, "Musical Events," *New Yorker*, 3 March 1951, 103.

84. Contract between Urban Nagle, O.P. and Warner Brothers Pictures, Inc., 3 July 1951, Nagle papers.

85. Francis Cardinal McIntyre, Letters to T.S. McDermott, O.P., 16 July 1951, Nagle papers.

86. Information on the dispute between Nagle and Carey is based on the following letters in the Nagle and Carey papers in the Dominican Archives, Washington, D.C.: Urban Nagle, O.P. to: T.S. McDermott, O.P., 26 March 1951, 11 June 1951 and 2 August 1951; John J. McManus, n.d.; "Mal," 11 November 1951; "Gertrude," n.d. Thomas Carey, O.P. to T.S. McDermott, O.P., 12 February 1951 and 31 August 1951. T.S. McDermott, O.P. to: Urban Nagle, O.P., 31 March 1951, 19 September 1951 and 15 January 1952; Thomas Carey, O.P., 13 February 1951 and 19 September 1951; Gerald Tyne, 13 February 1951; Robert Healy, 21 September 1951. Gerald Tyne to T.S. McDermott, O.P., 27 January 1951, 6 February 1951, 13 February 1951, 24 May 1951, and 28 August 1951. John J. McManus to: Robert Healey, 19 January 1952; T.S. McDermott, O.P., 2 March 1951. Robert Healey to T.S. McDermott, O.P., 19 September 1951.

87. Thomas Carey, O.P., to T.S. McDermott, O.P., 12 February 1951, Carey papers.

88. T.S. McDermott, O.P. to Gerald Tyne, n.d. (written in response to a letter of August 1951), Nagle papers.

89. T.S. McDermott, O.P., to Urban Nagle, O.P., 19 September 1951, Nagle papers.

88. T.S. McDermott, O.P., to Thomas Carey, O.P., 19 September 1951, Carey papers.

90. Father Urban Voll, O.P., interview with the author, 22 November 1996.

CHAPTER 4
THE MIDDLE YEARS: 1952-1960

Father Carey now had to face the prospect of operating the Blackfriars theatre without the creative contributions of Father Nagle. Fortunately Nagle had previously seen the need for additional personnel for the theatre. In 1951 Nagle had asked Father Terence McDermott, O.P., the provincial, for one or two young priests to join the work at Blackfriars. Nagle even offered to pay the tuition for the training of the priests out of Blackfriars' funds. Consequently McDermott told newly-ordained Father Robert Alan Morris, O.P., who had an interest but no formal training in theatre, that he would be studying at the Yale School of Drama.[1] Nagle had suggested to Morris that he study technical theatre and in the fall of 1951 Father Morris began studies at Yale.

Dennis Gurney, although a close friend of Nagle's, stayed on at Blackfriars and continued to direct. Floyd Allan, who had previously designed three productions for Blackfriars, continued to do sets and lighting for all of the theatre's plays until 1952.[2] Allan, although trained primarily as a scene designer, supported himself as an interior decorator. He received roughly $500 for each production he designed. Several different people handled costumes for the theatre between 1952 and 1960, but two people designed most frequently. Irene Griffin, who had begun doing costumes for the theatre with *Lady of Fatima* in 1948, designed for Blackfriars until 1954. And Bill Griffin costumed all Blackfriars' shows from 1957 to 1960. Carey hired Mollie Carroll as a full-time secretary for the theatre, but he handled all of the financial aspects of the theatre himself. A part-time custodian completed the staff.

Blackfriars still had no difficulty getting actors for its productions. Father Morris estimated that as many as 500 hopeful actors auditioned for each production during this period. Many were non-Equity actors hoping to be seen by agents and directors. Blackfriars always provided free tickets to actors so that they could invite agents as well as friends. Others were Equity actors between shows who used assumed names. Among the young actors who auditioned for Blackfriars during this period were Charlton Heston, Ben Gazzara and Pat Carroll.[3] Perusal of audition sheets from this period also reveals a growing number of television actors. The resume of one typical actor, for example, lists credits in *The Big Story, Danger, Armstrong Circle Theatre, The Philco Playhouse, Studio One, You are There* and *Ellery Queen*. Carey also began to emphasize the "showcase" aspect of Blackfriars and to use a double cast. Each play had a first and second cast with the second cast acting as both understudies and alternates. This allowed actors who got a paying role the freedom to leave on short notice. It also enabled television actors who might have a single performance on a live telecast to miss a performance. The theatre, in fact, guaranteed alternates they would have six or seven performances during the six week run of the play so that they could invite agents.

Blackfriars generally produced only two plays a season because of the rising cost of production and also because there was a greater chance of making a profit if they could run a production longer. Since the theatre was not air-conditioned there were no performances in the summer. And since Carey didn't feel that he could ask non-salaried actors to perform over the holidays, they scheduled no performances over Christmas and New Year's. The usual procedure was to open one play sometime in October and perform it until early or mid-December, depending on audience demand. The second play opened in February and ran until Holy Week. The time of Holy Week varied from year to year and, if there were sufficient audiences, the play might be re-opened after Easter.

After being closed for almost thirteen months, the Blackfriars re-opened its theatre in April 1952 with *The Restless Flame*, a dramatization of the life of Saint Augustine, by Louis de Wohl. De Wohl was a German-born writer of historical and religious novels. He adapted the play from his novel of the same title. Dai Keong Lee, who co-authored *Open the Gates*, wrote the incidental music for the production. Jim O'Connor of the *Journal-American* was restrained, but positive in his review. He called the play "inspiring" and said it "was enacted by a large cast of surprising competence."[4]

Carey realized the difficulty of producing a play by himself. During the summer he asked Morris not to continue his degree program at Yale and to join the staff of Blackfriars in the fall. Morris consented and Father McDermott gave his permission. Carey also asked McDermott to send another priest to get a theatre education, since Morris was not the addition that he was intended to be but was only a replacement for Nagle. Carey needed someone with an expertise in playwriting so McDermott sent Father Dominic Rover, O.P., who had shown a talent for writing, to study playwrighting at Yale.[5] Carey envisioned Rover's role at Blackfriars as searching for appropriate scripts, editing and revising scripts and, if necessary, writing plays.

Morris stated that his first impression of Blackfriars after joining the staff was arriving at the theatre after small casting notices had been placed in *Variety* and other trade papers.

> The first day I came to the theatre it was 1:00 in the afternoon, the date of casting. There were something like two hundred and fifty actors and actresses sitting out in the theatre waiting to fill out applications and get lined up for auditions. I was utterly amazed, just couldn't believe it. I couldn't believe that all these people were willing to sign up for several weeks for nothing.[6]

Morris realized later the motivation of all those actors and actresses.

> To find a place like ours where they could get into a show and run a few weeks and really get a part down and have many opportunities for somebody to see them was a great boon for them.

A romantic comedy about a New England spinster and a sea captain, which opened the 1952-53 season, was the first Blackfriars production Morris worked on. *Faith and Prudence* by Lottie Michelson was "inferior stage material," wrote the reviewer for the *Times*.[7]

The second play of the season was a play that Carey had asked

Father Brendan Larnen to write. Larnen was teaching at Providence College in Rhode Island at the time. It was the beginning of Carey's practice of "plays by prescription." Carey wanted a play about the life of Saint Thomas Aquinas, the thirteenth century Dominican theologian and philosopher. Aquinas lived the life of a quiet scholar, so Larnen chose a few dramatic highlights from his life: his capture and imprisonment in the family castle to prevent him from joining the Dominicans, his brothers' attempt by means of a courtesan to dissuade him from his religious vocation, his fight with the officials at the University of Paris and his composition of the Office of Corpus Christi. Working with these facts, Larnen welded in some fiction and supposition about the courtesan. Carey, however, wanted more theological statements from the scholarly works of Aquinas included in the play. He told Morris that "to the best of his knowledge the five proofs for the existence of God by Thomas had never been done on stage."[8] Morris argued that "perhaps the reason it hadn't been done on the stage was that it belonged more in the pulpit or the classroom." Not dissuaded, Carey had several conferences with Larnen who acquiesced and included the topics Carey wanted. Larnen stated, however, that when he produced the drama himself at Providence College he took out the theological and philosophical material because "it just slowed down the play."[9] Despite some unnecessary verbage, Jack Shanley of the *Times* said that *Angelic Doctor* "is an intelligent and refreshing approach to a cloistered subject".[10]

Blackfriars opened the 1953-54 season with *Late Arrival*, a comedy by Charles Oxton. Oxton was public relations director for the University of San Francisco as well as a freelance writer. The central character of the play is a nineteen year old college girl, campaigning for the need for women to elevate themselves above their routine functions of housewife and mother. Her campaign is upset when her mother becomes pregnant and eventually gives birth to a son. By the end of the play the girl is engaged to be married and is planning a family of her own. The cast included John G. Williams as the girl's boyfriend.[11]

It proved popular with audiences. The *Journal-American* said "there is a certain freshness and enthusiasm that transmits itself to the audience" and called it "a gentle and innocuous little comedy."[12] "John G. Williams," the review continued, "is an engaging and competent young leading man." Samuel French, Inc. bought the acting rights and published *Late Arrival*.

The program for *Late Arrival* announced Blackfriars' next production, an as-yet untitled life of Saint Thomas More by actor-playwright John McGiver. Carey had commissioned McGiver to write the play.[13] After McGiver finished the first draft of the play, he met with Morris and Rover who suggested some changes. Rover was coming down from Yale on weekends to work at Blackfriars. After McGiver completed the changes, Rover and Morris suggested further changes. Finally, McGiver said, "You're asking me to write your play, not mine." Blackfriars then paid McGiver the fee agreed upon and Morris and Rover decided to write their own life of Saint Thomas More. Since they had already advertised a play by John McGiver, the two priests decided to use the pen-name, John McGuire. The play, entitled *Praise of Folly*, focused on the last days of Thomas More and especially his conflict with King Henry VIII. Rover and Morris took the risk of writing the play in blank verse and it proved to be one of the best written plays Blackfriars ever produced.

In the Blackfriars production Robert Harding played Thomas More, Mark Voland played Henry VIII, James Milhollin played Thomas Cromwell and Jayne Heller was Anne Boleyn.[14] Jack Shanley of the *Times* said *Praise of Folly* is "a drama of great dignity and power and a splendid theatre tribute to a remarkable man."[15] In regard to the verse, Shanley stated that "Mr. McGuire's verse is not stilted; it has majestic quality that makes his story soar and sing in its finer moments." John McClain of the *Journal-American* wrote that "The Blackfriars Guild lit up their little show shop . . . last night with *Praise of Folly*."[16] McClain called it "a thoughtful and engaging Off-Broadway effort, competently written and acted." Robert Coleman of the *Daily Mirror* referred to the play as "an accurate and interesting play about a learned and devout man. It is a moving and stimulating play."[17] Coleman also had high praise for the cast. Vernon Rice of the *Post* wrote that "much praise can be heaped upon *Praise of Folly* today. The John McGuire play . . . should be one of the Blackfriars' biggest successes."[18] Louis Sheaffer of the *Brooklyn Eagle* stated that

> John McGuire has done a highly commendable job of locating a human being inside the legendary figure of Sir Thomas More. . . . Ably directed by Dennis Gurney, *Praise of Folly* continually dramatizes the conflict of

Father Urban Nagle, O.P., founder of the Blackfriars Guild.

Cavada Humphrey and Augustin Duncan in *A Man's House* by John Drinkwater (1943).

Eileen Heckart and Gene Lyons in *Moment Musical* by Charles Angoff (1943).

Ruth White plays a poor white tenant paying her black landlord in *Caukey* by Thomas McGlynn, O.P. (1944).

David Kelly and Liam Dunn in *Career Angel* by Gerard M. Murray (1943), the first play to move from Off-Broadway to Broadway.

Come Marching Home by Robert Anderson (1946).

Trial by Fire by George H. Dunne, S.J. (1947).

Lady of Fatima by Urban Nagle, O.P. (1948). Edward Villela as Francisco is second from the right.

Peggy McCay and Darren McGavin in *On The Seventh Day* by Urban Nagle, O.P. (1947).

Grant Williams and Sheila Fallon in *Late Arrival* by Charles Oxton (1953).

City of Kings by Urban Nagle, O.P. (1949). Anthony Franciosa is second from the left.

Armor of Light by Urban Nagle, O.P. (1950) with Geraldine Page, third from the left.

Robert Harding, Iola Lynn and Kathy Phelan in *Praise of Folly* by John McGuire (Dominic Rover, O.P.) in 1954.

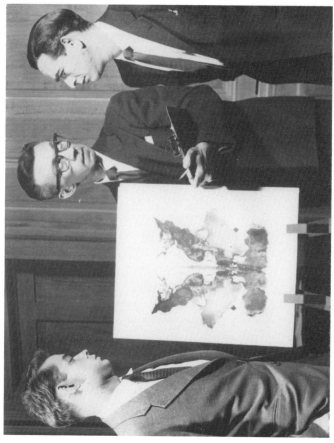

Gerald Campbell, James Milhollin and Shelley Berman in *Slightly Delinquent* by Leo Thomas (Dominic Rover, O.P.) in 1954.

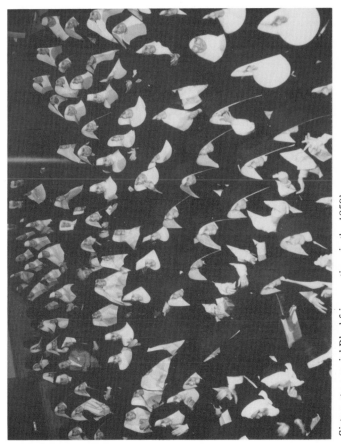

Sisters at a special Blackfriars matinee in the 1950's.

Curtain call for *The Red Hat* by Maureen Martin, Blackfriars' last production in 1972.

royal politics and religion in personal terms, a clash of personalities and fortunately it has players with the necessary amount of conviction and force."[19]

Twelve daily and weekly newspapers reviewed the play and gave it a completely favorable press.

To open the 1954-55 season Blackfriars produced *Slightly Delinquent*. The play satirized on modern psychological methods of treating juvenile delinquents. The play stemmed from an idea of Father Rover who was the son of a judge. He and Morris wrote the play during their summer vacation. The play concerned a judge's son who, mistaken for a juvenile delinquent, is put through the juvenile detention system. The cast included Shelley Berman as a newspaper reporter investigating the juvenile correction system and James Milhollin as a psychiatrist.[20]

The *World-Telegram and Sun* said: "The Blackfriars Guild has come up with a comedy which ranks as top drawer for the theatrical quality and entertainment value. . . . Its humor bites hard without ever becoming difficult to take or in questionable taste."[21] The reviewer added that "Shelley Berman is first rate as a hard-bitten reporter." Arthur Gelb, reviewing for the *Times*, wrote that "the Blackfriars Guild hit on a happy change of pace last evening. . . . Proving to be quite at home in a lighter vein, the Roman Catholic experimental troupe has staged a laugh-provoking, if slightly uneven, play."[22] Gelb pointed out James Milhollin's "endearingly wacky quality that lifts the role out of the stereotype it could easily have been," and called Shelley Berman's performance "entertaining." Shortly after the play opened, Blackfriars received a letter from Columbia Pictures expressing interest in the play and asking for a copy of the script. Nothing came of the inquiry, however.

Anticipating the spring production, Carey had again commissioned a script. He wanted a play about Maryknoll missionary sisters in China and he asked Sister Maria del Rey of Maryknoll to write such a script.[23] Sister Maria del Rey had written several books of fiction and non-fiction set in the Maryknoll missions, but had never written a play. After attempting the play, the nun told Rover and Morris that she was unable to work with the dramatic form. Rover, who joined the staff full-time in January, 1955, took over the task and wrote *Bamboo Cross* under the name Theophane Lee. The conflict of the play centers on Mark Chu, a young Chinese boy, who has been a good friend and pupil of the Sisters. He becomes convinced for a time that the Communists have the right answers to China's problems and goes over to their side. He is appalled, however, at the brutality of the Communist commissar who tries to make the Sisters confess to crimes against the Chinese people. In the end, he loses his life in his effort to help the Sisters escape.

Carey went to the Transfiguration Catholic School in New York's Chinatown to cast the one Chinese child who appears in the play. John Lee, a Chinese-American student at Saint John's College, was cast as Mark Chu. And Miriam Colon played a Chinese Catholic mother and friend of the Sisters.[24]

William Hawkins said the play "is economically written, timely and dramatic. It is, furthermore, extremely well acted."[25] Hawkins singled out Lee who, he said, "gives a stirring account of the young man." John McClain wrote that "it is given careful production: the direction and acting are first rate; authorship is credited to Theophane Lee, about whom I knew nothing beyond the fact that he can write a compelling scene."[26] Bob Francis wrote that *Bamboo Cross* is "timely and occasionally quite arresting" and "a rousing melodrama that engenders no little suspense."[27]

The National Broadcasting Company later bought *Bamboo Cross* and produced it for television. John Ford directed and Jane Wyman starred as one of the young Sisters. Maryknoll Press also published the play.

The 1955-56 season was Blackfriars' fifteenth in New York and to celebrate it Carey decided to revive one of the theatre's most critically acclaimed plays, *Song Out of Sorrow* by Felix Doherty. The play, which dramatized incidents in the life of Victorian poet Francis Thompson, had been produced in December of 1941, but because of America's entry into World War II the production was not well attended. The *Times* said that "the choice could hardly have been a surer thing. It is a sensitively written work that is being expertly acted."[28]

In February, 1956, the theatre produced the first play that Father Rover had written using his own name. The play, *Age and Grace*, dealt with the problem of separating the religious neurotic from the mystic. It was the story of an earnest young priest whose misdirected zeal for the spiritual welfare of a local parish girl almost leads to a tragic end. Confined to a wheelchair because of polio, the girl gives indications of being a true mystic. She seeks the spiritual direction of the young priest who inadvertantly helps to develop a neurotic condition in her. The girl comes to believe that only through acts of mortification and physical suffering can she achieve peace with God.

The reviewer for *Variety* thought that "the play suffers from the almost impossible task of resolving the problem posed." The reviewer continued, "Considering the nature of the predicament, it is surprising and refreshing to find the play generously sprinkled with raillery and laughter."[29]

Blackfriars had produced several successful plays and was beginning to show a slight profit. Both Fathers Rover and Morris felt strongly that if the theatre was making a profit then the actors should be paid.[30] The original reason for not paying the actors was that the theatre had been operating at a loss. That no longer being the case, argued Morris and Rover, there no longer existed any excuse for not giving the actors a salary. In addition, they thought that the Church could not preach about the principles of social justice unless it applied the same principles to its own employees. Father Carey opposed this because he thought it was possible to recruit good actors without paying them and also because he wanted to use the profits to start a fund to build Blackfriars' own theatre. Blackfriars' own building was a dream of Carey, and even though he had no money for construction, he had an architect draw up plans and sketches. However, he reluctantly agreed to pay the actors on a trial basis. In September 1956 Morris contacted Actors Equity Association and Equity agreed to allow its members to appear in Blackfriars productions on a standard Off-Broadway contract. Equity salary for Off-Broadway was then about $35.00 per week.

Father Rover also realized that it was getting more and more difficult to acquire original scripts of a high calibre. He stated that too often they would be within a month of auditions and still did not have a play to produce. "You wouldn't believe the terrible plays that people brought us just because we were a Catholic theatre," he said.[31] Morris concurred,

Outside of the problem of money, I suppose the problem of scripts was the biggest problem we faced. . . . The major difficulty was that we had people who were very, very Catholic and not good playwrights and

some other people who were pretty good playwrights but not very
Catholic, even with a small "c." So it became an increasing problem. . . .
He [Father Carey] was prepared, I think, to do fourteen shows in a row
and just take the lives of the saints. He figured, "Well, there's a great
story here and a great story there. We'll do Saint Francis, and we'll do
Saint Mark, then we'll do Saint Christopher . . . and so on and so
forth."[32]

Since good original scripts on religious themes were not being
presented to them, they had been forced to the expedient of writing
their own plays, as in the case of *Age and Grace*, or to run the risk of
commissioning them, as in the case of *Angelic Doctor*. Rover wanted
to alternate original scripts with revivals. Carey was dedicated to the
ideal of presenting original scripts. As long as he had Father Rover
and Father Larnen, he felt there was no danger of ever being without
a script. Carey also wanted scripts that Blackfriars could call its own.
Morris said that "Father Carey's great hope and dream was that one
play was going to come in and would be a super-duper thing that
would then go to Broadway and then to Hollywood and from the
million dollars we'd make from it, we could really build our own
theatre."[33] The conservative Carey again, very reluctantly, agreed to
do revivals on a trial basis.

Blackfriars opened its 1956-57 season as an Equity company. Carey
put in a Saturday matinee to help cover the cost of salaries for the
actors. There had been no discussion, however, of using union stage
crews and Actors Equity had never mentioned the issue. The theatre
group also planned to present two plays that had been produced
before.

The Comedian by Henri Gheon opened the season. Gheon (1875-
1943) was a French playwright who had attempted to combine the
theatrical reforms envisaged by Jacques Copeau with the expression
of his newly awakened Catholicism. The result was a series of simply
staged popular religious plays reminiscent of the Middle Ages. The
play blends legend, history and humor to tell of the martyrdom of
Saint Genesius, patron of actors. Genesius, one of the most popular
players of fourth century Rome, is ordered by the Emperor Diocletian
to appear in a play which burlesques the ceremonies of Christian
baptism. To prepare for the part Genesius does extensive research on
Christianity so that he can get inside of the character he is to play, the

martyr Adrian. In the process Genesius comes to believe in Christianity. He announces his belief and the Emperor puts him to death. *The Comedian* had never been produced in New York.

In the Blackfriars production Tom McDermott played Genesius and Doris Belack appeared as Julia. Arthur Gelb of the *Times* said: "The laughs and sighs that are being wrung from playgoers at the Blackfriars are enough to warm the hearts of any acting troupe. And the troupe deserves it, for it is an attractive one, colorfully costumed against an elegant Roman setting, and serving up plenty of meaty drama garnished with comedy."[34] Gelb thought that the story of Genesius "is handled with a light touch and there is some particularly funny backstage dialogue among the members of the play within a play." Gelb also praised the acting of Tom McDermott. John McClain in the *Journal-American* called the play "skillfully mounted." "Tom McDermott," he said, "cast in the exacting role of Genesius, handles the assignment with assurance and skill." And Doris Belack, he added, "has some highly humorous moments of her own."[35]

In the Spring, Blackfriars presented Christopher Marlowe's *Doctor Faustus*, a play that Father Rover had long wanted to do. The group presented a shortened version and, as a curtain raiser, did a one act comedy-fantasy by Henri Gheon. *Parade at the Devil's Bridge* is a simple story of a brief skirmish between a holy hermit, Father Kado, and the devil, disguised as a peddler, for the soul of a young village girl. The theatre presented the two plays under the title, *Two Tales of the Devil*.[36] The *Times* said: "The two plays complement each other felicitously and are expertly acted by a young troupe of players and excellently staged by Dennis Gurney."[37]

At the end of the season, Carey wanted to go back to the status quo.[38] He thought that paying the actors had not improved the calibre of the productions and had, in fact, put the theatre farther away from the reality of having its own building. He also wanted to go back to the production of original scripts. Morris and Rover felt equally strongly that the actors should be paid as a simple matter of justice. Blackfriars in fact did manage to operate in the black while paying its actors. Morris remembers. "We were paying our actors and we were still making money on it because the shows were doing very well." Rover stated that Carey, remembering the conflict with the unions in 1953, was afraid that with Equity actors they would eventually have to become involved with the crafts unions. Carey, always cautious, was also afraid that the lease on the theatre was going to be raised or that they might loose their lease altogether.

Furthermore, Morris and Rover both wanted to expand the perspective of the theatre. Morris envisioned Blackfriars as a Catholic cultural center. "Since we didn't play in the summertime and during Christmas and Easter we could also do other things -- poetry readings, lectures and seminars by critics and playwrights." Rover, in particular, wanted to go beyond the concept of religious plays. "I felt we should be free to find and produce plays which reflect life in our time, explore theological understanding of issues, or do plays which had the added investment of religious vision, like *The Tempest* for example."[39] And both Morris and Rover wanted to expand beyond the audiences composed primarily of parish groups from the suburbs who were bused in for the performances:

> It was our feeling that we had done as much as we could for the parish audience, and that if we were really going to make a contribution theatre-wise that it was the "non-saved" that we had to reach out to. Therefore to make this thing professional and good we couldn't count on amateur playwrights. We had to take good plays and get the best Equity actors in order to get the recognition of other people in the theatre. . . .
>
> Rover and I both felt it [the status quo] was really a step back, that we had done very well in what we were doing and not to go forward was to go backwards. We'd be putting overselves in a rut. We could stay in business and still have parish groups coming to see us and we would provide them with an evening's entertainment and even if we gave them any kind of edification or education, they were people who didn't need it for the most part. And to spend all that time and effort for just that postulate seemed to be missing the target.[40]

Carey insisted on his position, as did Morris and Rover on theirs. Finally they took the issue to Father William D. Marrin, O.P., who was now provincial superior. Father Marrin attempted to get the three priests to resolve their differences. Carey remained adamant, however. Morris and Rover felt it would be a waste of time, energy and talent to return to the way things had been. Seeing no way out of the impasse, the two younger priests offered to resign. Rover said, "We had basic differences. We felt if we can't resolve these things we'd rather leave. It was very painful to him [Father Carey]. It was very painful to us."[41]

Father Morris revealed that several lay people who were active in the theatre had the impression that the priests were being transferred against their wills and wanted to start a petition to keep them. Morris assured them that he and Rover were leaving by choice. In September 1957 Father Marrin assigned both Morris and Rover to the faculty of Providence College.

Carey had now resigned himself to running the theatre by himself, convinced that his direction was the right one. Carey's narrow vision of Blackfriars and his unwillingness to compromise would prove to be the downfall of the little theatre. In the fall Blackfriars returned to producing original scripts with non-salaried actors. Carey opened the next season, 1957-58, with *Truce of the Bear* by Pat Wilmot, a newspaper reporter who had also written short stories. This was Wilmot's first play and he set it in a narrow street in Budapest during the Hungarian Revolution of 1956. Carey hoped the play would be timely and popular because the Hungarian Revolution of the previous year was still fresh in people's minds. He was also happy to be able to make a statement about communism. Fred Scollay, later active in several Blackfriars productions, played one of the leads.[42] The play did not have the success Carey had hoped for. According to the critic for the *Times*,

> Mr. Wilmot, in his anxiety to get his ideas on the record, has failed to create on the stage the men and women who might have made his play live. Instead of the human struggle we are given little more than talk--about the fallacies of communism, the need for love in the world, etc. . . . . Mr. Wilmot, unfortunately, has confirmed his theatrical excitement to the battle taking place in the wings. On the stage he is too full of words.[43]

Blackfriars' next production was more successful. *The King's Standards* by Costa Du Rels had played for two hundred performances at the Theatre du Vieux Colombier in Paris in 1955. Du Rels was a Bolivian-born Frenchman who had written several novels and plays. *The King's Standards* told the story of the Worker Priests movement which began in France in 1943 in a desperate effort to win back the workers to the Church and to combat the strong influence of communism in the factories. The movement sought to have priests live and labor alongside workers in industrial areas and become a Christianizing influence. Despite its good intentions and the sacrifices of the priests involved, the movement was not a success and it came

under mounting criticism from both clergy and laity. The Vatican
dissolved the movement in 1954. Set in a working class rooming
house, *The King's Standards* concerns the response of two worker-
priests to the Vatican ban. One decides to defy the ban and stay
among the workers; the other makes the equally painful decision to
obey. Paul Eaton and Emmet Bain portrayed the two priests and
Richard Slattery their worker friend.[44] Fred Scollay directed. The drama
critic for the *Herald-Tribune* wrote,

> It is not often one sees such a lucid study of a struggle of conscience as
> in this intensely played Blackfriars production. . . . The internal
> struggles of these two men are lifted to a considerable pitch of tension.
> Whichever way one's sympathy may lie, one will find himself drawn
> into the struggle to an unusual degree.
>   For all the poignancy which this play possesses, it has many flashes
> of genuine humor.[45]

The critic for the *Daily Mirror* said the play "has tensely dramatic
moments, leavened with occasional flashes of humor."[46] The *Daily
Mirror* praised the acting and directing and added that "*The King's
Standards* is the kind of play usually considered non-commercial by
Broadway managements, but it is one well worth producing." The play
was popular enough that Samuel French, Inc. published it.

The program for *The King's Standards* announced Blackfriars'
production of *Child of the Morning* by Clare Booth Luce. Carey had
met Mrs. Luce, a convert to Catholicism, through Father Nagle. Carey
thought that the production of a play by Luce, author of the very
successful *The Women*, would be an artistic coup for Blackfriars.[47] He
hoped it would be the "hit" that might result in a new building for
Blackfriars. The play had previously been scheduled for a Broadway
production in 1951, but had been withdrawn for revisions during its
Boston try-out. Before Mrs. Luce found time to make the necessary
alterations she became involved in Dwight Eisenhower's presidential
campaign and later became United States Ambassador to Italy. Luce
allowed Carey to give the play its first New York production, though
she had never revised the script. Luce got the idea for the play from
the story of Maria Goretti, a young Italian girl who was canonized a
saint in 1950. Raped and repeatedly stabbed, Maria Goretti lived long
enough to forgive her attacker. Using the same concept, Luce set her

play in contemporary Brooklyn.

The completely negative reviews the play received shattered Carey's hopes. John McClain of the *Journal-American* said,

"This is a straggling and pretentious effort, the first such I have encountered at the Blackfriars . . . . The tale is told in a relentless and meandering manner, and it isn't much of a yarn to begin with. One of the reasons the show never reached Broadway originally was that it defied fixing and the complaint still stands. . . . It is a dismal evening, off-Broadway or on."[48]

Frank Ashton of the *World-Telegram and Sun* called the play "literarily spastic."[49] Walter Kerr of the *Herald-Tribune* wrote that "family and friends seem violently one-dimensional and the hand-wringing, powdered hair performances of the balance of the cast do nothing to make them breathe a little easier between religious crises or even to breathe at all."[50] Even the Catholic press was not supportive. Richard Hayes of *Commonweal* commented that "*Child of the Morning*, for all its high ardor of sanctity, suffers by being almost wholly the fruit of insistence, of a conscious effort of the will to do the work of the imagination."[51]

The problem of acquiring good scripts did not get any easier for Carey and the Blackfriars, as the 1958-60 seasons exemplified.

In the 1958-59 season Blackfriars produced *Listen to the Quiet* and *La Madre. Listen to the Quiet* by Fred Scollay, who had previously both acted and directed at the theatre, was a drama about the heroic resistance of a group of people against tyranny in an unnamed atheistic dictatorship. Critic Louis Calta commented: "The author's lack of character shadings, his formal and contrived method of writing reduce the script to rather amateur status."[52] *La Madre* was written by Sister Mary Francis, P.C., a cloistered nun from New Mexico. Set in sixteenth century Spain, it told the story of Saint Teresa of Avila and her heroic efforts to reform the Carmelite Order against resistance from inside and outside the Church. The *Times* said that the play "sacrifices the theatrical viewpoint for that of the pulpit . . . it is less inspired theatre than inspirational sermon."[53] Despite the play's lack of critical success, Samuel French, Inc. published it, hoping perhaps for a market among amateur Catholic groups.

In the 1959-60 season Blackfriars presented *The Egoists* and

Madame Lafayette. Carey had high hopes for the *The Egoists*, one of the few plays written by Francois Mauriac, French Catholic novelist who had won the Nobel prize for literature in 1952. It had never been performed in the United States. It was the story of a domineering father who manipulates the lives of his two daughters for his own selfish motives. The *Times* said: "In *The Egoists*, the author's attempt to give his characters flesh and blood fails miserably."[54] *Madame Lafayette* was the first effort of Catherine Hughes, twenty-four year old public relations director for Sheed and Ward publishers. It dramatized the life of Adrienne de Lafayette, the wife of General Lafayette of the American Revolution. Drama critic Lewis Funke said of the play: "In playwrights, as in revolutions, ambition can outstrip capacity."[55]

In the middle of the 1959-60 season Father Carey fired Dennis Gurney who had been directing for the theatre since 1941. Rover stated that Gurney's increased drinking caused more and more absences from the theatre and affected the quality of his work.[56]

Although there were internal conflicts at Blackfriars during the 1950's, its image among American Catholics couldn't have been better. Catholic publications pointed to the Blackfriars as an outstanding example of Catholic involvement in the arts. In 1954 *Sign* magazine did a feature story on Blackfriars and one of its regular actresses, Iola Lynn.[57] In 1955 *Christian Family*, in an article entitled "Theatre With a Purpose," declared that "the Blackfriars Guild in New York does a service to the stage of the nation."[58] And in 1956 *Catholic Preview of Entertainment* stated that "the Blackfriars Guild Theatre is one of the most remarkable [Off-Broadway theatres] for its experimental innovations and staying power."[59] In 1959 Carey used an interview in *Ave Maria* as an opportunity to publicize Blackfriars' "need" for a new theatre building.[60]

Father Carey's dream of a new theatre never became a reality. Just keeping the theatre operating would prove to be a struggle.

1. Father Robert A. Morris, O.P., interview by author, 19 January 1982.

2. Information on designers and actors is from various play programs and a tape recording of Father Robert A. Morris, O.P., Blackfriars Collection, Providence College Archives, Providence, R.I.

3. Information about auditioners from the Blackfriars Collection, Providence College Archives.

4. Jim O'Connor, "An Inspiring Play, Competently Acted," *New York Journal-American*, 15 April 1952.

5. Father Dominic Rover, O.P., interview with author, 20 January 1982.

6. Father Robert A. Morris, O.P., recollection, tape recording, n.d., Blackfriars Collection.

7. J.P.S. "Blackfriars Guild Presents a Comedy," *New York Times*, 15 October 1952.

8. Morris, recollection.

9. Father Brendan Larnen, O.P., interview with author, 12 May 1983.

10. J.P.S. "Blackfriars Stage Play About Aquinas," *New York Times*, 14 April 1953.

11. Shortly after *Later Arrival*, John G. Williams began using his middle name. As Grant Williams, he appeared in the films *Written on the Wind,Susan Slade, PT-109* and *Doomsday*. From 1959-63 he starred in the television series, *Hawaiian Eye*. Williams is probably best remembered for playing the lead in the 1957 science fiction classic, *The Incredible Shrinking Man*.

12. John McClain, "Gentle Little Drama," *New York Journal-American*, 20 October 1953.

13. Father Dominic Rover, O.P., interview with author, 10 May 1983.

14. A union member, Herb Voland acted at Blackfriars under the name Mark Voland. Voland later appeared as a character actor in many "B" level films, such as *With Six You Get Egg Roll, The Love God*, and *The Shakiest Gun in the West*. He also played the recurring role of General Clayton in the television series, "M*A*S*H." James Milhollin had previously appeared in *Angelic Doctor* at Blackfriars and later appeared as the psychiatrist in *Slightly Delinquent*. Milhollin's portrayal in the latter earned him the role of psychiatrist in the Broadway production of *No Time for Sergeants*. Milhollin has made a career as a character actor in television and films. Jayne Heller left the cast of *Praise of Folly* during its run to play in *Sabrina Fair* on Broadway.

15. J.P.S., "At the Blackfriars," *New York Times*, 24 February 1954.

16. John McClain, "The Theatre," *New York Journal-American*, 24 February 1954.

17. Robert Coleman, "The Theatre," *New York Daily Mirror*, 24 February 1954.

18. Vernon Rice, "Curtain Cues," *New York Post*, 24 February 1954.

19. Louis Sheaffer, "Theatres," *Brooklyn Eagle*, 26 February 1954.

20. Shelly Berman went on to a sucessful career in theatre, television and film. He is best known, however, for his highly popular stand-up comedy routines and his comedy recordings. Actor Vic Morrow auditioned for the part of Angie, a juvenile delinquent, but was not cast.

21. William Hawkins, "Theatre," *New York World-Telegram and Sun*, 26 October 1954.

22. Arthur Gelb, "Theatre: Blackfriars," *New York Times*, 26 October 1954.

23. Rover, 10 May 1983.

24. Miriam Colon became very active in Hispanic theatre in New York. At this writing she is executive director of the Puerto Rican Traveling Theatre.

25. William Hawkins, "Theatre," *New York World-Telegram and Sun*, 23 February 1955.

26. John McClain, "Remarkable Drama About Modern China," *New York Journal-American*, 22 February 1955.

27. Bob Francis, "Bamboo Cross," *Billboard*, 5 March 1955.

28. Arthur Gelb, "Blackfriars Revives Doherty's Drama," *New York Times*, 1 November 1955.

29. Georg, "Age and Grace," *Variety*, 29 February 1956.

30. All information about the dispute over salaries for actors and original scripts is from personal interviews with Morris and Rover and from Morris' tape recorded recollections.

31. Father Dominic Rover, O.P., interview with author, 3 November 1982.

32. Morris, recollection.

33. ibid.

34. Arthur Gelb, "Theatre: *The Comedian*," *New York Times*, 18 October 1956.

35. John McClain, "The Comedian," *New York Journal-American*, 18 October 1956. Doris Belack became a successful supporting actress on stage and in television and film. She appeared in the daytime series, "One Life to Live" and has played the recurring role of a judge in "Law and Order." Her films include *Tootsie* and *Naked Gun 33 1/3*.

36. Actor Peter Falk's agent brought him to Blackfriars to audition for *Doctor Faustus*, but Gurney and all three priests thought him "inappropriate" for the play.

37. Louis Calta, "Double Bill of Demonology at Blackfriars," *New York Times*, 19 February 1957.

38. All information about the dispute between Carey and Morris and Rover is from personal interviews with Morris and Rover and from Morris' tape recorded recollections.

39. Rover, 20 January 1982.

40. Morris, recollection.

41. Rover, 20 January 1982.

42. Fred Scollay had appeared as an alternate in *Age and Grace*. He later directed *The King's Standards* and wrote *Listen to the Quiet* at Blackfriars. He became a supporting actor in television and films.

43. I.B.F., "*Truce of the Bear* at Blackfriars Guild," *New York Times*, 24 October 1957.

44. Richard X. Slattery later appeared in *Child in the Morning* and *Listen to the Quiet* at Blackfriars. Slattery subsequently appeared in such films as *A Distant Trumpet, The Secret War of Harry Frigg, The Boston Strangler* and *Herbie Rides Again*. He also portrayed the Captain in the television series *Mister Roberts*.

45. Paul V. Beckley, "Off-Broadway," *New York Herald-Tribune*, 14 February 1958.

46. Robert Coleman, "Blackfriars' Play Interesting," *New York Daily Mirror*, 15 February 1958.

47. Besides *The Women* and *Child in the Morning*, Luce wrote *Abide With Me, Kiss The Boys Good-Bye, Margin for Error* and *Slam the Door Softly*. She also wrote the scenario for the film, *Come to the Stable*. Luce was a war correspondent and served in Congress from 1943-47.

48. John McClain, "Dreary Effort by Mrs. Luce," *New York Journal-American*, 22 April 1958.

49. Frank Ashton, "Mrs. Luce Has a New Drama," *New York World-Telegram and Sun*, 22 April 1958.

50. Walter Kerr, "*Child of the Morning* on at the Blackfriars Guild," *New York Herald-Tribune*, 22 April 1958.

51. Richard Hayes, "The Stage," *Commonweal*, 9 May 1958, 153-4.

52. Louis Calta, "Blackfriars Offer *Listen to the Quiet*," *New York Times*, 28 October 1958.

53. Arthur Gelb, "The Theatre: *La Madre*," *New York Times*, 12 February 1959.

54. Louis Calta, "*The Egoists* Staged," *New York Times*, 14 October 1959.

55. Lewis Funke, "Blackfriars Present *Madame Lafayette*," *New York Times*, 4 March 1960.

56. Rover, 10 May 1983.

57. "Blackfriars Actress," *Sign*, June 1954, 37-39.

58. Ralph Land, "Theatre With a Purpose," *Christian Family*, February 1955, 2-5.

59. "The Blackfriars: Experiment in Good Theatre," *Catholic Preview of Entertainment*, December 1956, 56-58.

60. Catherine Hughes, "Show Business Showcase," *Ave Maria*, 13 June 1959, 5-9.

CHAPTER 5
THE FINAL YEARS: 1960-1972

The 1960's brought increased problems for Blackfriars. With the loss of Father Rover the acquisition of good scripts appropriate for Blackfriars, which had always been a problem, became critical. With increased Off-Broadway activity young playwrights had more opportunity for exposure. Blackfriars was not as attractive as it had been when young Robert Anderson wrote *Come Marching Home.* Father Carey's insistence on producing overtly religious plays with a clear moral only exacerbated the problem.

Since few, if any, playwrights were bringing good scripts to Blackfriars Carey relied more and more on the expedient of "commissioning" plays. He thought up ideas for plays, often on the lives of saints, and had them written by writers he knew and trusted. During this period he depended on four playwrights. One was Father Larnen, who had written for the theatre from the beginning and who wrote four plays for the theatre during this period. Another, Father Edward A. Molloy, C.SS.R., wrote his first play while recuperating from a heart attack.[1] Molloy also turned out four scripts for Blackfriars. Carey also encouraged Mary Drahos, a woman suffering from multiple sclerosis, to write plays both for her own benefit and Blackfriars'. Drahos produced three scripts for Carey. And Rose Grieco, a housewife from New Jersey whose plays had previously been rejected by Father Rover, had two plays produced at Blackfriars. Of these playwrights only Larnen showed the necessary skill and talent to write a successful play.

Father Rover once remarked that "the quality of plays was not important to Father Carey; it was the idea."[2] Elizabeth McCann, currently a Broadway producer who worked backstage at Blackfriars in the 1950's said: "It's never easy to find good plays, and if you're cautious about theme and content it's even more difficult. . . . He [Carey] seemed content with the lives of the saints."[3] Carey's insistence on explicity religious dramas and his practice of commissioning plays based on his ideas are seen in the plays Blackfriars presented from 1960 to 1972. Of the twenty-six plays produced, twelve were biographical dramas about saints, prospective saints, Biblical figures or other Catholic heroes: the Virgin Mary, Mother Cornelia Connelly, Mary Queen of Scots, Edith Stein, Oscar Wilde, Saint Alphonsus Liguori, Saint Patrick, Pope Pius XII, Saint Catherine of Siena, Pontius Pilate, Blessed John Ogilvie and Saint John Fisher. Six plays were farces or domestic comedies in Catholic settings. And six were "thesis plays" dealing with specific problems: abortion, the crisis of the modern priesthood, changes in the Catholic Church, teenage morality, priests and Sisters leaving their ministries, and women's liberation. Only two plays did not fall into one of these three categories. Carey preferred to stick with plays with safe, non-controversial subject matter and themes. Although the 1960's was a decade marked by the greatest civil rights movement for African-Americans since the Civil War and Blackfriars had an early history of supporting this cause, Carey never produced a play about racial justice. Likewise he ignored the moral dilemmas created by the Vietnam War.

Carey's own lack of an artistic sense compounded the problem of the lack of good scripts. Carey's training had been as a psychologist and he initially joined Blackfriars as a set builder, organizer and fund-raiser. In the first ten years of the theatre's operation, Father Nagle handled the aesthetic aspects. Later Carey relied on Father Rover, who had studied playwrighting at Yale. Alone, Carey clearly lacked the talent to recognize artistic quality. Elizabeth McCann commented: "My impression of Father Carey was that he was a kind, well-intentioned man, but that he was not particularly aesthetic. He could build a set, but I don't think he had a clue how to put any artistic or creative juices into that theatre."[4]

Carey also remained cautious and conservative in terms of the audience. He relied more and more on Catholic parishes from the suburbs who bussed in groups. Carey knew that he could depend on those groups for an audience for plays simply because the plays were Catholic. They almost guaranteed him audience. It appeared much safer than taking the risk of competing with other theatres for regular New York theatre-goers. It also did not force Blackfriars to expand beyond its traditional religious play. McCann stated: "There was no attempt made to stretch that audience. Nothing controversial was ever done. . . . Essentially Blackfriars was doing less and less exciting theatre." She added, "Sometimes you'd hear people talk about the way things had been when Father Nagle was there."[5]

Blackfriars was also experiencing greater competition from other Off-Broadway theatres. When Blackfriars opened in 1941, fewer than a half dozen similar groups existed in New York. In the 1960's there were over one hundred Off-Broadway productions a year.[6] Off-Broadway had become more sophisticated, with quality productions and standard Equity contracts for actors. The late 1950's and early 1960's brought the advent of Off-Off-Broadway where young actors and playwrights could gain experience and experiment with new theatrical forms, usually without pay. While Blackfriars had once surprised New York audiences with plays like *Caukey* and *Trial by Fire*, other groups were now presenting innovative theatre. Blackfriars still presented its traditional fare. These factors all diminished Blackfriars' role as an experimental theatre.

Blackfriars' reputation suffered as a result. In 1954, Bob Francis of *Billboard* had said of Blackfriars: "The group can keep taking bows as the town's best experimental theatre."[7] Comments by Dan Sullivan of the *Times* in 1968 indicate a marked difference in the attitude of the theatrical community:

> The Blackfriars Guild bills itself as "New York's oldest Off-Broadway theatre." It might be more accurately described as New York's-- and probably the nation's-- oldest Little Theatre.

> Here survive, slightly updated, the laundered and earnest melodramas that were the staples of American community theatre in an earlier, more innocent era. But they are doing Beckett in Toledo these days, and *Marat/Sade* in Seattle. You have to come to New York to see something like [Blackfriars's current play].

> That is, you would have to come here to see real live actors doing it. You

can see it on television any night of the week.[8]

Just as Blackfriars was now only one among many Off-Broadway theatres, it was also no longer the only church group involved in theatre in New York. In 1961 Al Carmines became assistant minister at Judson Memorial Church and soon after opened the Judson's Poets Theatre which produced innovative works on a wide variety of themes. There was never any assumption of church-imposed restriction on the nature of the material at Judson. Carmines stated,

> God can take care of himself. This is the first article of the Judeo-Christian religion: we don't have to protect God. We can do a decadent play or a cynical play that's totally nihilistic, with the feeling that we can be exposed to it without secret weapons--without having to think of some way in your mind of defending yourself.[9]

In 1964 the American Place Theatre, founded by Episcopal priest, Father Sidney Lanier, moved into Saint Clement's Church. Lanier wanted to assist both the theatre and the Church to deal more directly with "the crucial themes of contemporary life."[10] Through sharing a common building he hoped that the church and the theatre could enter into a dialogue. American Place/Saint Clement's opening production was *Old Glory* written by Robert Lowell, directed by Jonathan Miller and starring Frank Langella.

In 1963 the Second Vatican Council began and brought about sweeping changes in the attitudes and practices of Roman Catholics. Suddenly the insularity and cautiousness, which particularly characterized American Catholics, disappeared. The Counciliar Fathers, in *Guadium et Spes*, declared: "The Church, at once a visible organization and a spiritual community, travels the same journey as all mankind and shares the same earthly lot with the world: it is to be a leaven as it were, the soul of human society."[11] The theatre was not unaffected by the Council and by changing attitudes. The Council called the theatre a "pristine and honorable art" and said the theatre should "appeal to human aspirations and ideals."[12] Influenced by this new openness to the secular and no longer seeing any value in a separate Catholic theatre organziation, the National Catholic Theatre Conference dissolved itself in 1968.

From 1959, when Carey fired Gurney, until 1962 he relied on two directors, Michael Kray and Elton Ellsworth, to stage Blackfriars' plays.[13] From 1962 until 1971 Walter Cool directed all Blackfriars' productions--nineteen plays in all. The most frequent scene and lighting designer during this period was Allen E. Klein. Klein designed thirteen productions from 1960 to 1971. And Carey, who hadn't designed a set for Blackfriars since *Caukey* in 1944, designed for seven productions during this period, including *Eternal Sabbath*, *Reunion of Sorts*, and *Five Star Saint*. The *New York Times* called his set for *Eternal Sabbath* "utilitarian."[14]

During this period Blackfriars' productions ran for an average of forty-five performances. Rent on the theatre in 1964 had gone up to $11,000 a year, but this was still less than many Off-Broadway groups.

Blackfriars opened the 1960-61 season with *Shepherds on the Shelf* by Father John P. O'Donnell, a speech and drama teacher at Quigley Preparatory Seminary in Chicago. The play was a farce set in the recreation room of a home for priests who have been forced to retire. Samuel French, Inc. published the play, probably hoping for productions by Catholic boys high schools who needed a harmless comedy with an all-male cast. In the program for *Shepherds on the Shelf*, Blackfriars began advertising itself for the first time as "New York's oldest Off-Broadway theatre."

The spring production was *Connelly vs. Connelly* by Father Brendan Larnen, O.P. The original idea for the play came from a review of a biography of Mother Cornelia Connelly that Larnen read.[15] Coincidentally Carey later read the biography and presented the idea to Larnen as the subject for a play.

Cornelia Peacock Connelly, born in Philadelphia in the early nineteenth century and reared as an Episcopalian, married Pierce Connelly, an Episcopal minister, at the age of twenty-two. Pierce Connelly later converted to Roman Catholicism and his wife followed him into the Church. Mr. Connelly then decided that he wanted to be a Catholic priest. After gaining Cornelia's consent and providing for the upbringing of their three children, Mr. Connelly received a special papal dispensation for a marital separation and for him to enter a seminary. Pierce Connelly was ordained a Catholic priest in 1845. Meanwhile Cornelia responded to a request of Cardinal Manning of London and founded the Sisters of the Holy Child Jesus, a teaching order, and became their first mother general. Pierce Connelly later renounced Catholicism, however, and initiated a civil suit in England against Mother Cornelia, demanding restoration of his conjugal rights.

The play focused on that trial, with flashbacks to the events leading up to the case. In preparing the script, Larnen did extensive research on the case and also researched English legal practice of the nineteenth century. Adrienne Hazzard starred as Mother Cornelia.

The production gave Blackfriars its first critical success in three years. The *Journal-American* said it was a "clever play, well acted . . . a straightforward courtroom drama, thoughtfully constructed by Reverend Brendan Larnen, O.P. Direction by Michael Kray is effective and unostentatious . . . it is a pleasant and provocative evening of theatre."[16] Frank Ashton of *World-Telegram and Sun* stated that

> the Larnen drama rates among the most moving I have ever seen in the little house. Speaking as a denominational outsider, I was profoundly moved. . . .Under Michael Kray's austere direction, the tale unfolds with calm power. . . . The final scene is especially effective. . . . As the wife, Miss Hazzard practically reduced emotional old me to tears.[17]

And the critic for the *Times* commented that "for much of the three acts it is interesting . . . but then in the last act it becomes exalting . . . and lyrical. . . . As played by Adrienne Hazzard, she [Mother Cornelia] is serene and noble."[18] The play ran for eighty performances, a record for Blackfriars up to that point.

The 1961-62 season almost duplicated the previous one -- a comedy followed by a biographical play about a religious figure by Father Larnen. *Anthony on Overtime* by Rose Grieco told of an Italian-American matron with a special devotion to Saint Anthony and a propensity for matchmaking. *My Beginning* was the story of the last days of Mary, Queen of Scots and her conflict with Elizabeth I of England. The play focused on Mary's steadfast adherence to Catholicism. Though essentially Larnen's idea, he wrote the play because Carey did not have a play for the Spring. *Backstage* commented that, in the play, "probing and piercing questions of the strength and depth of orthodox faith are asked and answered. No one could leave this play without being touched and moved by Mary's valiant struggle."[19]

In the fall of 1962, Carey hired Walter Cool to direct the first musical play that Blackfriars had done since *Open the Gates* in 1951.

Although a graduate of the Cincinnati Conservatory of Music, Cool worked full-time for Kraft Foods.[20] He was the first director at Blackfriars without training in the theatre. After his first directing assignment at the theatre, Carey asked Cool to stay on and he directed for Blackfriars until 1971.

During Cool's first season, Blackfriars produced three plays for the first time since 1957-58. None received favorable reviews from the critics. *Lady of Mexico* was an operetta about the apparition of the Virgin Mary to an Indian in sixteenth century Mexico. Sister Mary Francis, P.C., who had written *La Madre*, wrote the book; and Father Joseph Roff, an Italian-born priest who had studied music at Cambridge University, England, composed the music. *Backstage* said: "A potentially dramatic and exciting story has been slowed down to a crawl by amateurish writing, unimaginative staging and music which is uninspired. The actors move stiffly and unconvincingly as the plot plods wearily on."[21] Despite that negative response, G.I.A., Inc., of Chicago, publishers of church music, published the operetta under the title, *Counted as Mine.*

Decision at Tongo by J. J. Geoghegan was based on the massacre of twenty Holy Ghost missionaries in the Congo in 1962, and treated the conflict of Christianity and Marxism in Africa. *Daddy Comes Home* was a comedy extolling the simple things of life that Rose Grieco wrote at the request of Father Carey.

To open the 1963-64 season Carey wanted a play about Edith Stein. Edith Stein (1891-1942), German Jewish philosopher and assistant to Edmund Husserl, converted to Roman Catholicism in 1922. She continued teaching and writing until anti-Semitic laws forced her from her teaching position in 1933. That same year she entered the cloistered Carmelite nuns at Cologne. In 1938, because of increased Nazi oppression and her own denunciation of German treatment of the Jews, her superiors moved her to a Carmelite convent in Holland. However, in 1942, as a reprisal for an outspoken pastoral letter of the Dutch bishops condemning persecution of the Jews, she was arrested along with other priests and nuns of Jewish ancestry. The Nazis sent her to the concentration camp at Auschwitz where she died in the gas chamber. Admirers of Stein initiated the cause for her canonization.

Carey asked Mary Drahos to write a biographical play and the result was *Eternal Sabbath*. Drama critic Louis Calta called the play "a touching and ironically amusing drama despite considerable artless-

ness in the craftsmanship."[22] "Artlessness in craftsmanship" was a
term that Calta applied several times to plays at Blackfriars. Calta
added that "what saves the play from skittering all over is the quiet
dignity brought to it by the dedicated actors. They achieve a genuine,
spiritual fervor." Maureen Martin, a playwright who worked at
Blackfriars in the early 1970's, observed that the high calibre of the
acting generally consistent at the theatre redeemed several poorly-
written plays.[23]

Blackfriars' second production of the season was another
biographical play -- about Oscar Wilde's last days at the Hotel
d'Alsace in Paris and his deathbed conversion in 1900 to Catholicism.
Carey had first asked Larnen to write the play and when Larnen
declined because of lack of time, Carey asked Father Edward A.
Molloy, C.SS.R., a Redemptorist priest then recuperating from a heart
attack. Molloy had never written a play before.[24] Molloy based his
play, *Finis for Oscar Wilde*, on the written statement of Father
Cuthbert Dunne, C.P., an Irish priest of the Passionist Order who
received Wilde into the Church. Dunne had kept silent about the
incident for many years, but his superior persuaded him to write down
his recollections before he died in 1950. *The London Magazine* finally
published the account in 1961. In the hands of a more experienced
writer, the play might have succeeded. However, Jack Thompson of
the *Journal-American* noted "the drama is saved for the last few
moments and an extremely talky two hours precedes it." The actors,
he said, "are earth-bound by the dialogue assigned them."[25]

Early in 1964 *The Deputy* by Rolf Hochhuth opened in New York.
The play portrayed Pope Pius XII as an accomplice of the Nazis in the
persecution of the Jews. Carey, like most Catholics, felt strongly that
the play presented a completely false and slanderous portrayal of
Pius. Coincidentally, Father Molloy, who had written *Finis for Oscar
Wilde*, had long been a student of the life and works of Pius XII.
Molloy had studied all twenty-two volumes of the writings and
speechs of Pius, as well as his forty-three encyclicals. Carey therefore
asked Molloy to write a play to counter-act Hochhuth's image of Pius
and to present the facts accurately. Molloy spent several months
reading dozens of histories and biographies as well as examining
pertinent documents. He then wrote *The Comforter*, a docu-drama
about Pius XII's efforts to save the Jews during World War II. Molloy
subtitled the play "A Reply to *The Deputy*."

The Comforter received more press coverage than any other play Blackfriars had produced. Several newspapers outside New York, including Los Angeles, Cincinnati, and Providence, either reviewed the play or reported it.[26] At least four European publications printed stories about the production: *Der Spiegel* and *Mannheimer Morgen* in Germany, *Epoca* in Italy and *La France Catholique* in France.[27]

The reaction of the American press was mixed. Joseph Casey of the *Jersey Journal* wrote,

> One might have expected that Blackfriars Guild's production to be a more obsequious apologia for Pius XII. Instead, last night's audience was given a powerfully understated etching of a giant of our age. Father Molloy's *The Comforter* is not the dramatic vehicle that *The Deputy* is, but it is far more worth seeing than the latter.[28]

Martin Gottfried of *Women's Wear Daily* offered a quite different appraisal.

> The theatre is hardly the choicest place for a debate-- dramatic sense is more important to a play then forensic strength. . . . As a play it [*The Comforter*] has all the weaknesses as theatre and debate that a staged argument is bound to have. . . . As a playwright Father Molloy ignored plotting-- understandable under the circumstances but bad for the stage. His act structure is awkward. But he is a polished playwright. His dialogue is smooth, his arguments strong. His personal beliefs may be too intense for the play's good, but the result was genuine stimulation and an important argument. . . .
>
> Pius is treated adoringly and sacredly. He becomes a sanctimonious, boastful man, describing his own greatness. Only in a single scene, alone and praying for divine guidance does Pius seem human.[29]

However, the harshest treatment of the play came from a Catholic publication, *Our Sunday Visitor*, in an article that appeared two days before the production opened.

> I know it's only fair to let a show open before blasting it with both barrels. However one opens Tuesday evening that will, I'm afraid, set our so-called Catholic Theatre back a decade or two. . . . I'm afraid it's going to make Catholics look silly in the eyes of their friends.

Not that we should care what others, friends or foes, think of us, if we're right. But here's a case where I feel we're wrong. . . .

What I'm trying to say is that one just doesn't write a play "in answer to" something. One preaches a sermon, scrawls a polemic, pens an essay, etc. But a play isn't a tool and those who consider drama as a tool to be used to peddle some particular proposition-- whether it be soap or sanctity-- evidence a total misunderstanding of what drama is. . . .

The play as described can't be the work of poetic or dramatic art, but at best a slam-bang piece of rhetoric. The idea seems to be "we'll show 'em." But we're not showing anybody anthing except that "our side" is prostituting art in the same way that Hochhuth did.[30]

Despite such a negative reaction, enough busloads of Catholic parish groups patronized *The Comforter* so that it ran for sixty-two performances.

The second production of the season was in marked contrast to *The Comforter*. *Patrick the First*, a charming comedy-drama by Father Larnen, received a good press and broke Blackfriars' attendance record. Larnen based the play on legends about the life of Saint Patrick. The *Times* said, "Father Larnen has interspersed his religious drama with the mischievous humor and charm of the Irish."[31] The play was so popular with audiences than it ran for ninety performances.

An unfortunate choice, *Mackey of Appalachia*, opened the 1965-66 season. Walter Cool, a native of West Virginia, wrote the musical comedy which he set in rural Appalachia in 1900. Leo Mishkin of the *Morning Telegraph* said the production "may be best described as something falling between the New England of *Carousel* and the Dogpatch of *Li'l Abner*, but falling way, way behind."[32] Mishkin referred to the production's "naivete and even amateurishness," and said it is the "sort of thing you expect from the annual show put on by the men's club and ladies auxiliary of your local parish."

Unfortunately reviews like Mishkin's became all too common for Blackfriars productions. An examination of reviews of Blackfriars by the *Times* from 1966-68 indicates consistent dissatisfaction with the productions.

The Man Who Washed His Hands by William C. Thompson (Winter,

1967): As we watch this devoted but not exceptionally talented cast struggle along in their home-made costumes and home-made set, we feel positively nostalgic for C. B. DeMille. . . .

The Happy Faculty by Joan and Philip Nourse (Spring, 1967): Its cast . . . is stiff and amateurish. . . . One only wishes the authors' perfectly valid insights were laced with a little wit.

Guimps and Saddles by Father Edward A. Molloy, C.SS.R. (Fall, 1967): Molloy has pressed the stage into service more as a vehicle for soul-searching than for drama.

Babes Don't Cry Anymore by Michael Kallesser (Spring, 1968): Except that it has been done so often before, the play might be interesting (in a horrible sort of way). . . . The cast . . . is on the amateurish side.[33]

These reviews point out the apparently declining quality of Blackfriars' productions and also the prevalence of "moral messages" in the plays.

The generally negative attitude of the critics apparently caused Carey to feel somewhat bitter and alienated from the New York theatrical community. In an interview Carey stated, "The commercial theatre is not a damn bit interested in what we do."[34] And in a program note Carey stated: "Today theatre (and the cinema) is an anything-goes game based on the almighty dollar."[35] He also revealed his disappointment that the playwrighting program of the drama department at Catholic University, which he helped to start, had not presented any scripts to Blackfriars. He specifically mentioned that Jean Kerr, one of the department's most famous alumna, had not offered a play to the theatre. Father Rover mentioned that Carey was also disappointed that Walter Kerr, formerly of the faculty of Catholic University and a colleague of another Dominican, Father Gilbert V. Hartke, O.P., was not supportive of Blackfriars.[36] In fact, as drama critic for the *Herald-Tribune*, he only reviewed one Blackfriars production-- *Child of the Morning* by Clare Booth Luce. It was also the only time Kerr came to a Blackfriars play.

In the fall of 1968 Blackfriars finally produced a modest success. The play, *The Ballad of John Ogilvie* by Father Ernest Ferlita, a Jesuit priest studying at the Yale School of Drama, was a dramatization of the trial and execution of seventeenth century Scottish Jesuit priest, Blessed John Ogilvie, by the Protestant government. Ferlita had researched the play in Scotland and based the drama on Ogilvie's own account of his arrest and trial which he managed to smuggle from prison and on the official transcript released by the government. Michael Diamond portrayed Ogilvie. The *Times* said that the play is "a little long on histrionics and a little short on new perspectives, but a creditable effort on the whole." Diamond, it stated, "interprets the role of Ogilvie manfully and heroically."[37] In the spring of that same season the theatre presented *The Priest in the Cellar* by Father James S. Conlon, professor of speech communication at Saint Joseph Seminary in Yonkers, New York. The play tells the story of a priest who tries to hide from his ministry and the effort of several diverse people to persuade him to return. Though the play ran for forty-two performances it did not receive positive reviews.

Since there were efforts in several states in 1969 to legalize abortion, Carey asked Mary Drahos to write a play about abortion. She wrote *Reunion of Sorts*, the story of two women with different views on abortion who meet again after many years in a New York hospital room. *Reunion of Sorts*, though strongly anti-abortion in tone, was a dramatic departure for Carey's tenure at Blackfriars in that one of the women does have an abortion. Later, however she regrets what she has done. Even Theophilus Lewis, in the Catholic magazine *America*, wrote: "The author is obviously biased and her play is more special pleading than dramatic."[38]

Blackfriars' next play was the fourth effort by Father Molloy and his most successful one. *Five Star Saint* dramatized the last days of Saint Alphonsus Liguori, eighteenth century Italian founder of the Redemptorists, the order to which Molloy belonged. Having founded the Redemptorists in 1732, Liguori later served as a bishop and wrote devotional, theological and moral works. Afflicted with poor eye-sight in later life, he was tricked into signing a document which resulted in the splitting of the order into two separate factions. He found himself excluded from the society he had founded and did not live to see its reunification. The *Times* said:

> "It is no mean feat to write a good play-- one of words, ideas and theological concern without an iota of visible action-- about a good man obsessed with the idea of doing good. Such a play, as written by Reverend Edward A. Molloy, vibrated thoughtfully and, at its best, succinctly, on the stage of the Blackfriars."[39]

In October 1970, shortly before the theatre's next production, *Transfiguration* by Father Larnen, was to open, Father Carey had exploratory surgery. The surgery revealed inoperable and terminal cancer. Doctors were unsure exactly how long Carey had to live. Larnen took over supervising the production of his own play. *Transfiguration*, set in the framework of a publishing company, concerns an ex-priest and an ex-nun, now husband and wife, and their book which tells of their experiences before and after leaving the ministry of the Church.

Carey showed no signs of abandoning the work of Blackfriars and seemed determined to carry on until the last. Maureen Martin stated that many lay people who were active in the theatre questioned why Father Carey made no efforts to recruit younger Dominican priests to take over Blackfriars.[40] Perhaps, Carey, not having been able to work with Nagle, Morris and Rover, preferred to continue alone, or that he did not trust younger priests. Father Larnen suggested that Carey knew that, given the changing circumstances in the theatre and the Church, time was running out for Blackfriars.[41]

At any rate, Carey returned to produce *And the Devil Makes Five* by Walter Cool in February, 1971. The play told the story of one man who contacts the devil to beg compassion for humanity when the world is on the brink of nuclear war. The quality of the acting again appeared to have redeemed the production from the poor writing.

In the summer of 1971, Walter Cool's company transferred him to the Midwest and the ailing Father Carey found himself without a director. Carey asked Fred Scollay, who was then appearing on the daytime televison serial, *Somerset*, for help in finding a director. Scollay recommended Jerry N. Evans. Evans, a former college drama instructor, had acted professionally and was then working as a stage manager for television. Coincidentally, Evans had auditioned for Blackfriars in 1956. Evans recalled the difference between the Blackfriars he remembered in 1956 and the Blackfriars he encountered in 1971: "There was incredible activity then [1956]. . . . My surprise was how musty it was [in 1971]. . . . It was sort of pathetic. There didn't seem to be any life in the place."[42] Blackfriars paid Evans approximately $750 for each production he directed.

Evans' first directing effort was the fall production of what would be Blackfriars' last season. The play, *Lib Comes High* by Joan T. Nurse, drama critic for the *Catholic News* of New York, used a cast of only three. It focused on a woman's alienation from the Catholic Church and her attempt to deal with a woman's place in society. Evans, who had no voice in the selection of the script, called *Lib Comes High* "very thin material," and said "it was like a half-hour television script made into a full-length play."[43] Evans also related that he had difficulty working with Carey. "I had some troubles with him; he was so used to being the authority. . . . He wanted everybody to participate. His attitude was more community theatre. I wasn't interested in that. I generally ignored him." Evans felt that Carey's illness allowed him greater freedom to direct in his own way. Evans also remembers Blackfriars' audience as being "mainly older people."

While *Lib Comes High* was in performance, Carey asked Maureen Martin to write the second play of the season. Martin had joined the work at Blackfriars in 1969 when she became coordinator of radio and television for the Catholic Archdiocese of New York. Martin had written for radio, but had never attempted a play. Carey suggested a biographical play about Saint John Fisher, a contemporary of Thomas More. Fisher, one of the few English bishops to oppose King Henry VIII, was imprisoned and later beheaded. While in prison, however the pope made him a cardinal, much to the anger of Henry. Martin called her play *The Red Hat*. Blackfriars paid Martin $500 for the play and an additional $500 for assistance she gave during the production.

In late December, 1971, before auditions for *The Red Hat*, Carey learned that the building that Blackfriars had occupied since 1941 would be torn down to make room for a new high-rise office building.[44] The owners allowed Blackfriars to occupy the theatre only until the summer. With Carey dying and the loss of the theatre the fate of the Catholic theatre group seemed sealed.

Both Evans and Martin remembered the atmosphere of Blackfriars' final production as "grim."[45] Carey's health got much worse and it was evident to everyone that he was dying. Carey had always made it a point to greet audiences before each performance as well as at intermission. Martin said that during performances of *The Red Hat*, Carey would come to the theater each night to greet the audience and then lie down on a cot in a back room to regain the strength to greet the audience again at intermission. Martin also added that previously Carey would always be the last person to leave the theatre. As his illness worsened, he went home as soon as the last audience member left.

Ironically, *The Red Hat*, the group's last production, was, in critical terms, the best production Blackfriars had staged since *Connelly vs. Connelly* in 1961. Howard Thompson of the *Times* called Maureen Martin "a gifted new playwright." Thompson pointed out the many similarities to *A Man for All Seasons* and said,

> Wonder of wonders, the new play then emerges in the wake of that other spectacular success as a separate entity with plenty to say on its own. . . . Miss Martin has devised a perceptive, compassionate and trenchantly ironic conversation piece in two succinctly organized acts. With its quick, wry thrusts of dialogue, and some good acting, the play is a keenly stimulating evening of theater. . . . Next to the playwright, credit should go to the firm, unobtrusive direction of Jerry N. Evans.[46]

A week after the play closed, Ted Mann of Circle-in-the-Square Theatre, came to see a run through of the play and to consider it for possible production at Circle-in-the-Square. While Mann liked the play, he did not think it appropriate for his theatre.[47]

The Red Hat had its final performance on March 26, 1972 and in April Blackfriars began the painful procedure of moving out of the theatre where they had been for thirty-two years. Six weeks after the final curtain, May 8, 1972, Father Carey died. Maureen Martin speculated that Carey got his wish and died with the theatre.[48]

Reminiscing years later, Maureen Martin said,

> I can see Father Carey emerging from the little room at the back of the house at show's end -- stooped, in pain, and not rested despite the cot, but determined to carry on, smile at departing patrons and bid us all "good night." It was the passing of an era when he died.[49]

Without a theatre and a priest to act as moderator, fund-raiser, producer, etc., there was little hope for keeping the theatre in operation. Maureen Martin and about a dozen others who had been active in Blackfriars formed a group called The Friends of Father Carey and made an effort to keep Blackfriars going. Father Kenneth Sullivan, O.P., provincial superior of the Dominicans, did make some token efforts to interest Dominican priests with training in theatre to take over supervision of the group. None, however, were interested. Father Larnen speculated that, in the eyes of many Dominicans, Blackfriars had become the special personal mission of Carey rather than a ministry of the Order.[50] Another factor was that in the ecumenical atmosphere after Vatican II, many young priests seriously questioned the validity of separate Catholic organizations and activities. Larnen also pointed out the difficulty of finding another theatre space that Blackfriars could afford. Father Raymond Daley, O.P., who was then assistant to Father Sullivan, recalls that from their standpoint the motivation to close Blackfriars was "principally financial."[51]

Ironically, no one really made the decision to close Blackfriars. It would be more accurate to say that it died and that no one wanted, or was able, to resurrect it. The Theatre-by-the-Sea in Matunuck, Rhode Island purchased all of Blackfriars' equipment: seats, lights, scenery, properties and costumes. The files: scripts, photographs, programs, newspaper clippings, correspondence: were sent to the archives of the library at Providence College in Providence, Rhode Island. Providence College, also operated by the Dominican Friars, gladly accepted them.

Larnen stated that shortly before Carey died he had talked briefly about keeping Blackfriars operating as a publishing house for religious plays. Larnen decided to publish one of Blackfriars' more successful plays as a posthumous tribute to Carey. He chose his own play, *Connelly vs. Connelly*, which had run for eighty performances. It was the first and only play Blackfriars ever published.

The officers of the Blackfriars corporation actually did not meet to dissolve the organization officially until late 1975. The original articles of incorporation stated that, in the event of the organization's dissolution, the assets were to go to the Dominican Province of Saint Joseph. Before that, however, Larnen suggested that some money be donated to a theatrical venture of the Dominicans. Consequently, the corporation, with the assent of Father Sullivan, donated $40,000 to Providence College to be used for a theatre arts scholarship in memory of Fathers Carey and Nagle. The remaining money, about $200,000, went to the Province of Saint Joseph which used it to pay off a sizable debt it had incurred.

An experiment in Catholic theatre which had lasted thirty-two years came to an end.

1. Information on playwrights is primarily from personal interviews with Father Dominic Rover, O.P., 20 January and 3 November 1982 and 10 May 1983.

2. Rover, 20 January 1983.

3. Elizabeth McCann, interview by author, 21 April 1983. Elizabeth McCann, in conjunction with Nelle Nugent, has produced such Broadway successes as *Elephant Man, Morning's At Seven, Amadeus, Crimes of the Heart, The Dresser, Mass Appeal, The Life and Adventures of Nicholas Nickleby, 'night, Mother,* and *Good.*

4. McCann, interview.

5. McCann, interview.

6. Stuart W. Little, *Off-Broadway: The Prophetic Theatre* (New York: Coward, McCann and Geoghegan, Inc., 1972), 230.

7. Bob Francis, "Off-Broadway Shows," *Billboard,* 6 March 1954.

8. Dan Sullivan, "Theatre: *Babes Don't Cry Anymore,*" *New York Times,* 21 February 1968.

9. Little, 190.

10. Little, 234.

11. Fathers of the Second Vatican Council, *Gaudium et Spes* (Pastoral Constitution of the Church in the Modern World) in *Documents of Vatican II,* ed. Walter M. Abbot, S.J., trans. Joseph Gallagher (Baltimore: American Press, 1966), 239.

12. Fathers of Second Vatican Council, *Inter Mirifica* (Decree on Instruments of Social Communication) in *Documents of Vatican II,* 328.

13. Information about directors and designers is from various play programs, Blackfriars Collection, Providence College Archives, Providence, R.I.

14. Louis Calta, "Theatre: Blackfriars," *New York Times,* 19 October 1963.

15. Personal interview with Father Brendan Larnen, O.P., 12 May 1983.

16. John McClain, "Clever Play, Well Acted," *New York Journal-American,* 18 February 1961.

17. Frank Ashton, "Blackfriars' Play Based on Fact," *New Work World-Telegram and Sun,* 18 February 1961.

18. Milton Esterow, "Theatre: A Nun's Trial," *New York Times,* 18 February 1961.

19. Ernest Oppenheimer, "My Beginning," *Backstage,* 9 February 1961.

20. "West 57th Off Broadway," *The Kraftsman,* November-December 1965, 14-9.

21. Michael Berry, "Lady of Mexico," *Backstage,* 26 October 1962.

22. Louis Calta, "Theatre: Blackfriars," *New York Times,* 19 October 1963.

23. Maureen Martin, interview by author, 12 May 1983.

24. Larnen, interview.

25. Jack Thompson, "Drama Just Too Talky," *New York Journal-*

American, 15 February 1964.

26. The *Los Angeles Times*, the *Providence Visitor* and the *Cincinnati Post-Times-Star* were among the newspapers that ran stories on *The Comforter*. In addition *Staats-Zeitung und Herold*, the German-language newspaper for New York, reported on the production.

27. "Papst-Drama: Schwarze Bruder," *Der Spiegel*, 28 Oktober 1964. 18; R. B., "Entgegnung auf Hochhuths *Stellvertreter*," *Mannheimer Morgen*, 20 Oktober 1964. 20; Guido Gerosa, "Pio XII discute degli ebrei con Nenni," *Epoca*, 27 settembre 1964. 81-84; Georges Daix, "*Le Consolateur*: Une response au *Vicaire*," *La France Catholique*, 23 octobre 1964, 1-2.

28. Joseph Casey, "Vindicates Pius XII," *Jersey Journal*, 14 October 1964.

29. Martin Gottfried, "The Theatre," *Women's Wear Daily*, 23 October 1964.

30. John E. Fitzgerald, "One Bad Play," *Our Sunday Visitor*, 11 October 1964.

31. Louis Calta, "Play on St. Patrick at Blackfriars," *New York Times*, 19 February 1965.

32. Leo Mishkin, "Blackfriars' Failure," *New York Morning Telegraph*, 8 October 1965.

33. All reviews are from the *New York Times*: Edward B. Fiske, "Play About New Morality at Blackfriars," 12 October 1966; Dan Sullivan, "Pilate's Agony," 16 February 1967; Dan Sullivan, "New Kind of Campus Comedy," 19 April 1967; Richard F. Shepard, "Blackfriars' Guimps," 11 October 1967; Dan Sullivan, "Babes Don't Cry Anymore," 21 February 1968.

34. Father Thomas F. Carey, O.P., quoted in Robert Louis Hobbs, "Off-Broadway: The Early Years," (Ph.D. diss. Northwestern University, 1964), 387.

35. Program to *Transfiguration* by Brendan Larnen, O.P., Blackfriars Collection.

36. Rover, 3 November 1983.

37. Richard F. Shepard, "Theatre: Historical Tale," *New York Times*, 9 October 1968. Michael Diamond appeared in several Off-Broadway productions and later directed both Off-Broadway and regional theatre as well as in London.

38. Theophilus Lewis, "Reunion of Sorts," *America*, 18 October 1969, 342.

39. Howard Thompson, "Stage: *Five Star Saint*," *New York Times*, 12 February 1970.

40. Martin, interview.

41. Larnen, interview.

42. Jerry N. Evans, interview by author, 19 May 1983.

43. ibid.

44. Larnen, interview.

45. Martin and Evans, interview.

46. Howard Thompson, "The Theatre," *New York Times*, 24 February 1972.

47. Evans, interview.

48. Martin, interview.

49. Maureen Martin , interview by author, telephone, 3 December 1996.

50. Larnen, interview.

51. Father Raymond E. Daley, O.P., interview by author, telephone, 31 December 1996.

CHAPTER 6
WHY A CATHOLIC THEATRE?

As the previous chapter stated, several negative factors contributed to the demise of the Blackfriars Guild of New York. Changes in the Catholic Church after the Second Vatican Council caused many Catholics to question the validity of separate Catholic organizations and activities, including Catholic theatre. The growth of Off-Broadway diminished Blackfriars' unique position in New York. No longer one of New York's exciting experimental theatres, by the 1960's Blackfriars was just another Off-Broadway theatre at best, a peripheral community theatre group at worst.

One cannot deny too the fact that Father Carey's narrow attitude toward Catholic theatre and his resistance to change hindered the growth of the theatre and led to the production of religious plays of little or no artistic merit. Too many bad plays, such as *Anthony on Overtime*, *Reunion of Sorts*, and *Lib Comes High*, received productions only because they fulfilled the religious requirements Father Carey looked for. Added to this was his protective attitude toward the theatre and his failure to groom a replacement even when he knew he was dying.

The ambiguous attitude of the Dominican Order, more specifically the Province of Saint Joseph, also hindered the work of Blackfriars and at least contributed somewhat to its demise. Blackfriars had been from the beginning the idea and personal mission of Father Nagle, not of the Order. In the beginning the Order gave him permission to pursue his Catholic theatre work as long as he fulfilled his other full-time duties. During the first four years of the theatre's operation, Nagle directed Blackfriars while serving full-time at the *Holy Name Journal*. In a letter to his provincial superior in 1945, Nagle complained that "it was long understood that this nucleus of the most impressive opinion forming machine at our disposal was tolerated after hours and on 'free time.'" He added that "I thought that if my superiors wanted to regard as a recreational whim what I thought was an important cause, I'd keep it even on those terms."[1] It was shortly after that letter that the provincial allowed Nagle to work full-time at Blackfriars. Not until 1953, a year after he replaced Nagle as director of Blackfriars, was Father Carey relieved of his other duties at the Holy Name Society.

Even though the Dominican Order was ultimately the legal owner of the Blackfriars Guild, the Order never contributed financially to the theatre. In fact records indicate that Blackfriars annually made financial contributions to the Province of Saint Joseph.[2] For example, when the Dominican Friars were building a wing onto Saint Stephen's College, their school of philosophy for Dominican seminarians in Dover, Massachusetts, Blackfriars made a contribution to the construction. One can conclude then that the theatre was not in the same category as parishes, schools, foreign missions or religious publications which the Order financially assisted either directly or indirectly. If anything, at least some Dominicans looked upon Blackfriars as a possible source of income for its "real" apostolic and ministerial work.

Members of the Order did take pride in Blackfriars and, in a letter to Nagle in 1950, Father Terence S. McDermott, then provincial superior, wrote: "I am keenly interested in this activity [Blackfriars] . . . It is my wish that you continue producing plays under the auspices of Blackfriars."[3] And the Order did assign two young priests, Fathers Alan Morris and Dominic Rover, to assist Carey at the theatre, although the Order expected Blackfriars to pay for their education at the Yale School of Drama.

As time went on, Blackfriars became more and more the personal mission and ministry of Father Carey, although the Order encouraged it. However, when Carey died in 1972 the Order felt no responsibility to provide a replacement for him as it would for a pastor of one of its parishes or a principal or dean in one of its schools. Carey was sixty-nine years old at the time of his death and had been in poor health for almost a year. The Dominicans of the Province of Saint Joseph, however, made no effort to educate a young Dominican as his replacement.

However, despite its difficulties and failures, Blackfriars did make a significant contribution to the New York theatre because it served several important functions.

Blackfriars provided valuable experience and exposure for many young actors. A number, such as Geraldine Page, Eileen Heckart, Anthony Franciosa, Liam Dunn, Grant Williams, Patricia Neal, Ruth White, Richard X. Slattery, Darren McGavin, Shelley Berman and Doris Belack went on to very successful careers in theatre, film or television. Eileen Heckart noted that "there were seven [New York daily] newspapers then and they all reviewed the plays. I know it gave me exposure. To get a notice in a major New York paper then was something."[4] Geraldine Page credited Blackfriars with getting her a theatrical agent in New York: "Stephen Draper came to see *Armor of Light* and wrote next to my name on the program, 'that's somebody I could get work for.' He's been my agent ever since."[5] Other actors, while not gaining a national reputation, have had productive careers in Off-Broadway, stock and regional theatre. Actor Paul Meacham, who played Henry VIII in *The Red Hat*, remembers Blackfriars as a place where he improved his craft and gained confidence. He said, "I've used the review [of *The Red Hat*] in the *New York Times* and boasted about it being my first Off-Broadway role. Blackfriars was a well-known theatre then . . . The role was a boost for me, a stretching for me. I discovered that I could play large demanding roles. It helped me personally."[6]

Other veterans of Blackfriars have been successful in directing and producing. Miriam Colon became executive director of the Puerto Rican Traveling Theatre, Elizabeth McCann became a well-known Broadway producer and Jerry Evans became director of the daytime television series, *Ryan's Hope*. Evans stated, "I felt very honored to work there. I was pleased to say I directed there. It helped my career considerably. That review [of *The Red Hat*] in the *Times* was instrumental in my getting directing work in television. It gave some legitimacy to my career."[7]

Only one of Blackfriars' playwrights went on to a successful career in writing for the theatre. Robert Anderson, who wrote *Come Marching Home* (1946), later wrote *Tea and Sympathy, All Summer*

Long, Silent Night/Lonely Night, You Know I Can't Hear You When the Water's Running and *I Never Sang for My Father*. He also wrote the screenplays for *Tea and Sympathy, Until They Sail, The Nun's Story, The Sand Pebbles, The Night of the Generals* and *I Never Sang for My Father*. Louis Peterson, Jr. had two plays produced on Broadway and wrote television and screen plays, but his association with Blackfriars was as an actor in *A Young American* (1945). Clare Booth Luce, who wrote *Child of the Morning*, was already a well-established playwright when Blackfriars produced her play in 1958.

One of Father Nagle's purposes for founding Blackfriars was the encouragement of new plays "which reflect the spiritual nature of man and his eternal destiny." He envisioned Blackfriars as a showcase for new "Catholic" drama that would not have a chance in the commerical theatre. This proved to be one of the most difficult goals to fulfill. The paucity of good scripts which reflected the themes and values it wished to present always hampered Blackfriars. Father Carey's narrower view of Blackfriars' mission later exacerbated the problem.

It is true, however, that Blackfriars did produce plays of merit which might not otherwise have had a hearing. This was especially true in its first fifteen years of operation. Plays about racial justice, such as *Caukey* (1944), *A Young American* (1945) and *Trial by Fire* (1947) were courageous statements for the 1940's. Almost all the critics considered *Song Out of Sorrow* (1941 and 1955), *City of Kings* (1949), *Praise of Folly* (1954) and *The Red Hat* (1972) artistic achievements. Other foreign plays of merit, such as *The Comedian* (1956) and *The King's Standards* (1958) got their first American productions at Blackfriars.

In thirty years of operation only one play, *Career Angel*, had a Broadway production, and that one was not successful. *Career Angel*, however, did enjoy the distinction of being the first play to move from Off-Broadway to Broadway. Another play, *A Young American*, closed in Chicago during its out-of-town tryout. And the National Broadcasting Company produced *Bamboo Cross* for national television in 1955. Several plays, however, were published for amateur production. Dramatists Play Service published *Career Angel* and it became a favorite with Catholic boys' high schools. Samuel French, Inc. published *Seven Mirrors, Late Arrival, The King's Standards, La Madre* and *Shepherds on the Shelf*. Bruce Humphries, Inc. of Boston published *Song Out of Sorrow* and Farrar, Straus and Cudahy

published *Lady of Fatima*. G.I.A. Publishers of Chicago released the
operetta *Lady of Mexico* under the title, *Counted as Mine*. Nagle's
Savonarola was included in a collection of plays, *Theatre for
Tomorrow*, published by Longman Green and Co. Small Catholic
presses published other plays. Christopher Press released *City of
Kings* and the National Catholic Theatre Conference published
Bamboo Cross. And Blackfriars itself published *Connelly vs.
Connelly*. Through these publishers, thirteen plays which originated
at Blackfriars had subsequent productions, primarily at Catholic
colleges, high schools and parishes.

Ironically though, contrary to what Father Nagle thought, the
commercial Broadway theatre produced plays on religious themes
which had an impact both inside and outside the Catholic community.
Between 1941 and 1972, the years Blackfriars operated, Broadway
produced twenty-three plays with religious themes or with religious
settings. Most notable were *Joan of Lorraine*, *The Cocktail Party*,
The Potting Shed, *The Lark*, *J.B.*, *The Tenth Man*, *Becket*, *A Man for
All Seasons*, *Luther*, *Trial of the Catonsville Nine*, *Godspell* and
Jesus Christ Superstar.[8]

Blackfriars did serve as an example of Church and theatre relating
and working together. As the previous chapter stated, other church-
related theatre groups arose in the 1950's and 1960's, but Blackfriars
was an early pioneer as a religious theatre group. It functioned as an
important symbol in the New York theatre district of the fact that the
Church and the theatre did not have to be suspicious of and
estranged from one another. In fact, many who worked at Blackfriars
found the Church's involvement in theatre a natural one. Geraldine
Page commented that "it seemed natural to me that anyone, whether
they're Martians or whatever, would be involved in theatre."[9] Eileen
Heckart stated that "nothing Catholic was ever imposed on us. We
just knew that they [the Dominicans] were people who cared about
the theatre. After all, it's a form of communication. Why shouldn't the
Church be involved in it?"[10] Producer Elizabeth McCann said she
"wasn't surprised at priests running a theatre. It seemed natural
enough . . . like another of the Church's apostolates."[11] Director Jerry
Evans noted that Blackfriars was an example of "Catholic involvement
in the New York theatre. . . . Just the fact that it was Catholic oriented
served a function, like the Yiddish theatre."[12] Veteran actor Tom
McDermott, who played the lead in *The Comedian* in 1956, said, "The

theatre always suggests a temple to me. It seemed only right and proper that priests should be involved. . . . Blackfriars served a great purpose."[13] And actor Paul Meacham said, "It didn't strike me as odd that the Dominicans had a theatre. I studied theatre history and I knew that the theatre was reborn in the church, so why not? . . . I do remember that Father Carey prayed with the cast before the opening. I guess I just expected something like that. . . . My feeling was that the Dominicans love theatre."[14]

In addition Blackfriars functioned as an informal though often unintentional forum for the examination of questions of the relationship of religion and theatre. There was never a precisely worked out philosophy or theology of "Catholic" theatre at Blackfriars. It proved to be both one of its strengths and one of its weaknesses.

Father Nagle had defined Catholic theatre and Blackfriars simply as "theatre which reflects the spiritual nature of man and his eternal destiny."[15] In other words, Catholic theatre must, at least tacitly, recognize that the human is both a physical and a spiritual being with an immortal soul and that he or she is ultimately destined by God for eternal life in heaven. In practice, Nagle was willing to produce any play of artistic merit which did not contradict that view of humanity. Nagle did add the correlative that any subject could be treated in a play, but that any problem or conflict must be resolved in accordance with Christian principles. In other words, evil might be portrayed but it had to be clear that it *was* evil. Nagle, however, did not want to define Catholic theatre too precisely. In fact, he often preferred to speak of "theatre under Catholic auspices."[16] He once wrote, "Without attempting to define a Catholic play, either narrowly or broadly, we [Blackfriars] declared that any play which solved the problems it raised in accordance with Catholic principles . . . was grist for our mills."[17] Any play, then, not opposed to Catholic principles could be produced. Father Brendan Larnen stated that Nagle felt that, at least in theory, Blackfriars could produce any play that wasn't immoral.[18]

Nagle elaborated further on this broad view of Catholic drama in *Behind the Masque.*

There are many who regard as fit for Catholic theatre only the ecclesiocentric drama--the conflicts of those who are aware of grace and are fortified by the sacramental system. I'm almost falling into the trap of offering a definition of a Catholic play, but I must avoid that pitfall because, after twenty years of thinking it over, I haven't a pat definition.

We [Blackfriars] would like to offer that fare to those who want that fare. You have to play to audiences and consider to some degree what they will sit through, especially in the competition of New York. And if we built audiences for the ecclesiocentric play, we would be happy to supply those audiences. If success came our way, we would like to open one or twenty theatres dedicated to this type of drama. It is not goody-goody theatre at all. It merely takes the Catholic background for granted, as do Sigrid Undset's novels of medieval Norway. In point of fact, it removes a lot of difficulties. The author doesn't debate as to whether divorce or suicide (as a solution) is acceptable to his characters or his audiences. He knows they're not and everybody accepts that assumption. Likewise, the author can paint his villains as black as he wants (and his heroes as white) without offending any of the millions who shout "discrimination" at anyone who tries to write nowadays. All his characters are in the same boat and hold to the same basic principles.

That would be easy theatre, but from Blackfriars' point of view, it presents a certain weakness. We didn't set up to do a cross between dramatizations of the teaching of the Church and theatre. We set out to do theatre--a theatre embodying ideas.

To limit the appeal to those of one's convictions is to admit inability to bridge the gap and to sharpen sectarian lines. Theatre is no more sectarian than is essential catholicity. Nor could we handle some of the social problems we attempted if we said Catholic theatre is for and about Catholics. A case in point cropped up in one of our interracial plays. The author asked us if he should make his characters Catholic. We told him not to specify any religion. It is not a Catholic problem--as presented in the play. It is an American problem. To make the Negroes Catholics and the whites non-Catholics, or vice-versa, or to put them all in any one sect would have complicated and snarled the problem. It fit everybody as stated and was involved enough.

Then it would be a strain to inject religion into farce comedy and we didn't want to be barred from any dramatic form.[19]

Nagle also viewed theatre in the context of the Roman Catholic sacramentals.[20] Sacramentals are related to the Church's concept and doctrine of sacraments. The traditional Catholic definition of sacrament is an outward sign instituted by Christ to give grace.[21] Jesus Christ, then, instituted seven sacraments (baptism, confirmation, holy eucharist, penance or confession, anointing of the sick, marriage and holy orders) which use earthly, tangible elements and signs (water, bread and wine, oil, laying on of hands, etc.) to convey divine grace to man. Sacramentals, on the other hand, are tangible objects which are not in themselves channels of divine grace, but which may aid man in contemplating God and his saints and may draw the human being in the direction of divine grace. These sacramentals are most often images. Common sacramentals are crucifixes, statues, holy pictures and stained glass windows. The theatre, according to Nagle, might, under ideal circumstances, also serve as a sacramental-- a tangible, outward expression, drawing people to contemplate and confront spiritual realities. Had not the liturgical drama, asked Nagle, served such a function in the Medieval Church? Such a theatre, however, need not be explicitly religious. "Who can convince us more of the beauty of sacrifice than Rostand in *Cyrano de Bergerac*? Who brings us back to the love of simplicity more than J.M. Barrie? Or who points out the foibles of modernity more than some of Philip Barry's work?"[22] he wrote.

With this broad and imprecise definition of Catholic theatre, Nagle was able to produce plays on racial justice like *Caukey* and *Trial by Fire*, a play about politics like *Come Marching Home*, and a comedy with no religious trappings like *Derryowen*.

Father Carey, on the other hand, had a much more narrow and confining view of Catholic theatre and, consequently, of Blackfriars. For Carey the plays that Blackfriars produced should be didactic, should teach something. He frequently referred to "plays with a moral."[23] Playwright Maureen Martin, who worked at the theatre during its last two years of operation, stated that the morals or messages were often very obvious and even heavy-handed.[24] She and others in the company referred to these messages as "blue light specials" because Carey occasionally used special lighting effects for emphasis when the actors spoke the important "spiritual message." Carey's insistence on plays with a moral message of course affected the choice and quality of the plays at Blackfriars. Father Larnen remarked, "I often said to Father Carey, 'it might be teaching, but it's not a play.' He liked the spectacular, but he insisted on teaching."[25] This accounts for the fact that during Father Carey's tenure, especially during the latter half, Blackfriars presented a steady fare of plays about saints, prospective saints and Biblical figures, plays treating specific moral problems or innocuous comedies in Catholic settings.

Father Dominic Rover, who worked with Father Carey at Blackfriars from 1953-1957, stated that he never really believed in the work of Blackfriars, at least as it operated in those years. "I don't think I ever believed much in religious drama," he said years later.[26] He added that he worked in the confines of religious theatre because he had been assigned to do so and because Father Carey was in charge. Rover, like Nagle, preferred a broader, less confining view of Catholic theatre. He defined Catholic theatre as one "that is attracted to works of dramatic art that seem congenial in some way to the Catholic or Christian view of life."[27] The category would be a broad-ranging one:

> The directors of such a theatre might be attracted to a dramatic masterpiece that reflected in its own right some profound human values or insights. You might even want to do a production of *Oedipus* or *Macbeth* (a kind of ready-made morality play), or *The Tempest* (with or without pointing up the sublimating drive of the play in terms that suggest the transforming power of God). You might be attracted to a comedy, like Moliere's *Tartuffe*, that mocks false piety. A sensitive reading of *The Glass Menagerie* would fall under this "attraction", or the staging of a kind of authentic Christian work like *The Satin Slipper*, or the re-staging of a medieval morality play. Marlowe's *Doctor Faustus* could be considered, from this viewpoint, a kind of Christian morality play.
>
> Farce and satire would be very much within the scope of such a theatre; indeed, no dramatic form would be foreign to it. The principle of selection would be, in the end, the human and professional sensibilities of the producers. If they chose to be identified as "Catholics" and the theatre as a "Catholic" theatre, that would not be a misnomer.[28]

According to Father John Burke, O.P., formerly of the drama faculty of the Catholic University of America, both Nagle and Carey complained about their fellow Dominican friar, Father Gilbert V. Hartke, O.P.[29] Father Hartke was the founder and long-time chairman of the drama department of the Catholic University of America in Washington, D.C. Nagle and Carey had expected Hartke to channel actors and especially playwrights from Catholic University's well-known drama department to Blackfriars. It never happened. Carey was also disappointed that Walter Kerr, formerly of the Catholic University drama faculty and a friend of Father Hartke's, was not supportive of the Blackfriars. In Kerr's tenure as drama critic of the *New York Herald-Tribune* he only once covered a Blackfriars' play--and that resulted in his negative review of Clare Booth Luce's *Child of the Morning*. Father Rover stated that Carey had hoped that Kerr's wife, playwright Jean Kerr, would offer to script a play for Blackfriars. She never did.

Father Burke noted, however, that Father Hartke and others at Catholic University did not share Carey's or even Nagle's view of Catholic theatre. Father Hartke thought that there was no such thing as Catholic theatre. To him there was only one theatre--the commercial, non-sectarian theatre -- and Catholic University was concerned with preparing Catholics artistically and professionally to take their place in it. Hartke felt strongly that Catholics should try to be a positive moral influence in the "universal" theatre and not attempt to be separate from it.

Besides confronting questions of religion and theatre, Blackfriars provided a unique opportunity for the Catholic Church to minister to the personal and spiritual needs of theatre people. Saint Malachy's on West Forty-ninth Street was, of course, the official actors' parish, but Saint Malachy's depended upon actors and other theatre artists coming to the Church. With Blackfriars the Church went to the actors, as it were, and became involved with theatre people in their own milieu. Father Alan Morris stated, "We got involved in the lives and problems of the actors."[30] Father Dominic Rover said, "We did a lot of priestly work, counseling. Our presence was important. Morris and I had supper once a week at Downey's [Restaurant], where a lot of actors ate. We got to know a lot of them personally."[31] Actor Tom McDermott still remembers and appreciates Father Rover's compassion when McDermott's wife was undergoing serious surgery.[32] Actress Eileen Heckart became a Roman Catholic through her contact with the Church at Blackfriars, and Father Carey instructed her in the Catholic faith and received her into the Church.[33] Father Rover stated that he thought the Catholic presence in the theatrical world "was the most valuable aspect of Blackfriars."[34]

Finally, and perhaps most importantly, Blackfriars was significant simply because it was one more theatre--another place where playwrights could write, directors could direct, designers could design and actors could act. Actor Paul Meacham, who is not a Catholic, stated,

> I think it was wonderful that the Dominicans, the Catholic Church had a theatre because it was another theatre. If it adds another point of view, that's fine. I work in a field where perhaps two percent of the population sees it anymore. Some people feel that live theatre is almost an anachronism in our world. Everything is television and film. The fact is that the Catholic Church was a producer, had the money to produce plays, even if many of them were flops. Ninety percent of the shows in New York fail! Probably because the scripts aren't very good. It [*The Red Hat*] was one of the best plays that I've been in in New York. If you work in New York, you're in a lot of junk, junk written by famous people too. . . .
>
> I would argue against all Catholic message plays, but if you said, "Well, I guess then we won't have a theatre," I'd say, "No, have Catholic message plays but please have a theatre." That's my feeling about the death of Blackfriars. It was a loss.[35]

1. Urban Nagle, O.P. to T.S. McDermott, O.P., 17 April 1945, Nagle papers, Dominican Archives, Washington, D. C.

2. Blackfriars Collection, Providence College Library, Providence, R.I.

3. Letter, T.S. McDermott, O.P. to Urban Nagle, O.P., 12 October 1950, Nagle papers.

4. Eileen Heckart, interview by author, telephone, 19 October 1982.

5. Geraldine Page, interview by author, 20 October 1982.

6. Paul Meacham, interview by author, 13 May 1983.

7. Jerry N. Evans, interview by author, telephone, 19 May 1983.

8. This information was gleaned from: Daniel Blum, *Theatre World Annual*, vols. 1-28 [1944-72], (New York: Crown Publishers), and Daniel Blum, *A Pictorial History of the American Theatre, 1860-1976*, 4th ed., rev. by John Willis (New York: Crown Publishers, 1977).

9. Page, interview.

10. Heckart, interview.

11. Elizabeth McCann, interview by author, 21 April 1983.

12. Evans, interview.

13. Tom McDermott, interview by author, telephone, 15 May 1983.

14. Meacham, interview.

15. Urban Nagle, O.P., "Blackfriars Guild," privately printed brochure, n.d.. 1, Blackfriars Collection, Providence College Library, Providence, R.I.

16. Urban Nagle, O.P., *Behind the Masque* (New York: McMullen Books, Inc., 1951), 169.

17. *Ibid.*, 100.

18. Larnen, interview.

19. Nagle, *Behind the Masque,* 178-179.

20. Nagle, MS, "The Sacramentalism of Theatre," n.d., Nagle papers.

21. *Baltimore Catechism*, 23rd ed. (Buffalo: Rauch and Stoeckl, 1933), 69.

22. Nagle, "The Sacramentalism of Theatre."

23. Larnen, interview.

24. Maureen Martin, interview by author, 12 May 1983.

25. Larnen, interview.

26. Personal interview with Father Dominic Rover, O.P., 3 November 1982.

27. Dominic Rover, O.P., unpublished MS.

28. *Ibid.*

29. Father John Burke, O.P., interview by author, 10 May 1983.

30. Father Robert Alan Morris, O.P., interview by author, 19 January 1982.

31. Rover, interview.

32. McDermott, interview.

33. Heckart, interview.

34. Rover, interview.

35. Meacham, interview.

BIBLIOGRAPHY

Books

Abbot, S.J., Walter M., ed. *Documents of Vatican II*. trans. Joseph Gallagher. Baltimore: American Press, 1966.

Atkinson, Brooks. *Broadway*. New York: Macmillan Publishing Co., 1974.

Baltimore Catechism. 23rd ed. Buffalo: Rauch and Stoeckl, 1933.

Blum, Daniel, ed. *A Pictorial History of the American Theatre*, 1860-1976. 4th ed. revised by John Willis. New York: Crown Publishers, 1977.

Blum, Daniel and John Willis. *Theatre World Annual*. Vols. 1-28 (1944-1972). New York: Crown Publishers.

Brady, Leo. "Catholic Theatre Movement." *New Catholic Encyclopedia* (1966).

Brockett, Oscar G. and Robert R. Findlay, *A Century of Innovation: A History of European and American Theatre and Drama Since 1870*. Englewood Cliffs, N.J.: Prentice-Hall, Inc., 1973.

Coffey, O.P., James Reginald. *A Pictorial History of the Dominican Province of Saint Joseph*. New York: Holy Name Society, 1946.

Cogley, John. *Catholic America*. Garden City, N.Y.: Image Books, 1974.

Concilii Plenarii Baltimorensis II: Acta et Decreta. Baltimore: Joannes Murphy, 1868.

Concilii Plenarii Baltimorensis III: Acta et Decreta. Baltimore: Joannes Murphy, 1886.

Dorcy, O.P., Sister Mary Jean. *Saint Dominic's Family*. Dubuque: Priory Press, 1963.

Greenberger, Howard. *The Off-Broadway Experience*. Englewood Cliffs, N.J.: Prentice-Hall, Inc., 1971.

Guilday, Peter. *A History of the Councils of Baltimore, 1791-1884*. New York: Arno Press and New York Times, 1969.

_____. *The National Pastorals of the American Hierarchy, 1792-1919.* Westminster, Md.: Newman Press, 1954.

Hardon, S.J., John, ed. *Modern Catholic Dictionary.* New York: Doubleday and Co., 1980.

Hinnebusch, O.P., William A. *The Dominicans: A Short History.* Staten Island, N.Y.: Alba House, 1975.

_____. *The History of the Dominican Order.* Vol. I. Staten Island, N.Y.: Alba House, 1966.

La Beau, Dennis, ed. *Theatre, Film and Television Biographies Master Index.* Detroit: Gale Research Company, 1979.

Little, Stuart W. *Off-Broadway: The Prophetic Theatre.* New York: Coward, McCann and Geoghegan, Inc., 1972.

McAvoy, C.S.C., Thomas T. *A History of the Catholic Church in the United States.* Notre Dame, Ind.: University of Notre Dame Press, 1969.

McGill, Raymond, ed. *Notable Names in the American Theatre.* Clifton, N.J.: James T. White and Co., 1976.

Nagle, O.P., Urban. *Behind the Masque.* New York: McMullen Books, Inc., 1951.

_____. *Uncle George and Uncle Malachy.* Milwaukee: Bruce Publishing Co., 1946.

Price, Julia S. *The Off-Broadway Theatre.* New York: The Scarecrow Press, 1962.

Rigdon, Walter. *A Biographical Encyclopedia of Who's Who in the American Theatre.* New York: James H. Heineman, Inc., 1966.

Smith, Irwin. *Shakespeare's Blackfriars Playhouse.* New York: New York University Press, 1964.

Smith, S. *Notes on the Second Plenary Council of Baltimore.* New York: P. O'Shea Publishers, 1874.

Taubman, Howard. *The Making of the American Theatre.* New York: Coward McCann, Inc., 1965.

Tavard, George H. *Catholicism U.S.A.* New York: Newman Press, 1966.

Wilson, Garff B. *Three Hundred Years of American Theatre and Drama.* Englewood Cliffs, N.J.: Prentice-Hall, Inc., 1973.

Interviews

Burke, O.P., John. Personal interview. 10 May 1983.

Daley, O.P., Raymond E. Telephone interview. 31 December 1996.

Evans, Jerry N. Telephone interview. 19 May 1983.

Heckart, Eileen. Telephone interview. 19 October 1982.

Hinnen, James. Telephone interview. 19 October 1981.

Larnen, O.P., Brendan. Personal interviews. 18 January 1982 and 12 May 1983.

Martin, Maureen. Personal interview. 12 May 1983. Telephone interview. 3 December 1996.

Meacham, Paul. Personal interview. 13 May 1983.

McCann, Elizabeth. Telephone interview. 21 April 1983.

McDermott, Tom. Telephone interview. 15 May 1983.

Morris, O.P., Robert Alan. Personal interview. 19 January 1982.

Neal, Patricia. Telephone interview. 16 October 1996.

Page, Geraldine. Personal interview. 20 October 1982.

Rover, O.P., Dominic. Personal interviews. 20 January 1982, 3 November 1982 and 10 May 1983.

Voll, O.P., Urban. Personal interview. 22 November 1996.

Magazine Articles

"The Blackfriars: Experiment in Good Theatre." *Catholic Preview of Entertainment*, December 1956, 56-58.

Claudel, Paul. "The Catholic Theatre." trans. Adele Fiske, R.S.C.J. *Drama Critique* 3, no. 1 (1960), 6-10.

Driscoll, Richard. "Blackfriars Venture." *America*, 24 January 1942, 437-438.

Ferlita, S.J., Ernest. "The Church and the Theatre." *Drama Critique* 5, no. 2 (1962), 70-81.

Grady, S.J., Richard F. "The Theatre as a Weapon." *America*, 16 January 1932, 364.

Hayes, Richard. "The Stage." *Commonweal*, 9 May 1958, 153-154.

Hughes, Catherine. "Show Business Showcase." *Ave Maria*, 13 June 1959, 5-9.

Jordan, Elizabeth. "The Stage." *America*, 31 January 1925, 377.

Land, Ralph. "Theatre With a Purpose." *Christian Family*, February 1955, 2-5.

Larnen, O.P., Brendan. "God Takes the Stage." *Dominicana*, September 1937, 251-256.

Lavery, Emmet. "The Baby Walks." *America*, 25 September 1937, 593-594.

_____. "The Catholic Theatre: New Thought on Old Form." *America*, 5 December 1936, 197.

_____. "The Curtain Goes Up on the Catholic Theatre." *America*, 6 March 1937, 508-509.

_____. "The Parish Theatre." *Catholic Digest*, May 1938, 36-37.

Lewis, Theophilus. "The Stage." *America*, 18 October 1969, 342.

Lord, S.J., Daniel A. "Father Nagle and the Blackfriars." *Catholic Digest*, March 1947, 25-27.

O'Connell, Margaret. "The Dominicans on 57th Street." *The Torch*, January 1962, 16-19.

"Our Theatrical Sewers." *America*, 23 August 1930, 477.

"Questions and Answers." *Homiletic and Pastoral Review*, August 1936, 1188-1189.

Rover, O.P., Dominic. "The Concept of Christian Tragedy." *Drama Critique*, 1, no. 3 (1958): 2-10.

Savage, Courtenay. "Our Faith and the Footlights." *Catholic Digest*, January 1946, 28-32.

Skinner, R. Dana. "The Play." *Commonweal*, 24 December 1924, 189.

"The Stage." *America*, 10 May 1913, 112-113.

"Trial by Fire Stirs Audience to Boos and Tears." *Ebony*, June 1947, 104-110.

Windeatt, Mary Fabyan. "The Blackfriars Guild." *Sign*, December 1936, 285-286.

Wyatt, Euphemia Van Rensselaer. "The Drama." *Catholic World*, January 1925, 523.

_____. "The Drama." *Catholic World*, March 1929, 721-722.

Manuscript Collections

New York, N.Y. Theatre Research Library of the New York Public Library at Lincoln Center. Blackfriars Guild File.

Providence, R.I. Providence College Library Archives. Blackfriars Collection.

Washington, D.C. Dominican House of Studies. Archives of the Dominican Fathers and Brothers of the Province of Saint Joseph. The Papers of Urban Nagle, O.P. and Thomas Carey, O.P.

Newspapers

Backstage, 1971-1972.
Billboard, 1933-1958.
Catholic News, 1912-1922.
New York Daily Mirror, 1958-1963.
New York Daily News, 1952-1972.
New York Herald-Tribune, 1952-1966.
New York Journal-American, 1952-1966.
New York Post, 1960-1972.
New York Times, 1915-1972.
New York World Telegram and Sun, 1952-1966.
Show Business, 1971-1972.
Variety, 1952-1958.
Wall Street Journal, 1952-1955.

Dissertations

Hobb, Robert Louis. "Off-Broadway: The Early Years." Ph.D. diss., Northwestern University, 1964.

Keefe, Sister Mary Michael. "The National Catholic Theatre Conference: Its Aims and Achievements." Ph.D. diss., Northwestern University 1965.

Kelly, Michael Francis. "The Reaction of the Catholic Church to the Commercial Theatre in New York City, 1900 to 1958." Ph. D. diss., State University of Iowa 1959.

Panchok, Frances. "The Catholic Church and the Theatre in New York, 1890-1920." Ph.D. diss., Catholic University of America 1976.

INDEX

Babes Don't Cry Anymore (Kalles-
  ser), 108
Backstage, 103–4
Bain, Emmet, 92
The Ballad of John Ogilvie (Fer-
  lita), 108–9
Bamboo Cross (Lee), 85–86,
  120–21
Barbizon-Plaza Theatre, 35
Barrett, Roy, 41–42
Barry, Philip, 15, 17, 124
Barrymore, Ethel, 18
Barter (Nagle), 15
Behind the Masque (Nagle), 52
Behrman, S. N., 17
Belack, Doris, 89, 96n35, 119
"Believe Me If All Those Endear-
  ing Young Charms," 65
Bentley, Walter Edmund, 8
Bergman, Ingrid, 18
Berman, Shelley, 2, 85, 96n20, 119
Bernstein, Lester, 63–64
Bickford, Charles, 33
Billboard, 18, 58, 61, 69
Blackfriars Auxiliary, 51
Blackfriars Guild, 11, 16; back-
  ground of, 1–22; chapters, 15,
  22n59; founding, 14–17; incor-
  poration, 49n60, 113; publish-
  ing, 113, 121; purposes, 15–16,
  120
Blackfriars Guild Theatre. *See*
  Blackfriars Theatre
Blackfriars Institute of Dramatic
  Art, 14, 16
Blackfriars Theatre (Boston), 29
Blackfriars Theatre (London), 3
Blackfriars Theatre (New York),
  14; beginning, 23–50; final production, 111; final years, 98–
  117, 127; finances, 32, 45, 57,
  87, 89; founding, xii, 1; functions of, 119; growth, 51–79; li-
  censing, 27–28, 30–31; middle

years, 80–97; plays presented
  by, 99; seating, 30; staffing,
  80–81; theatre space, 24, 70,
  111–13. *See also specific pro-
  ductions, plays*
Blackfriars Theatre (Providence),
  37
Blackfriars Theatre (Washington),
  15
blacklisting, 35, 39–41, 52, 58
blacks, 68
Bolton, Whitney, 66
Boston Blackfriars, 29
Bradford, Ben, 29
Brady, Leo, 12
Broadway, xii, 18, 42, 121
Bronner, Edwin M., 54–55, 120
Brooklyn Tablet, 63
Brown, John Mason, 17
Bruce Humphries, Inc., 120
Buckley, Gerald, 58
Buckley, Jerry, 33
Burbage, James, 3
Burbage, Richard, 30
Burke, John, 125–26
Burtsell, Richard L., 7

Cabin in the Sky, 18
C.A.G. *See* Catholic Actors Guild
Cagney, James, 33
Calta, Louis, 29, 93, 104–5
Cardinal Hayes High School for
  Boys, 41
Career Angel (Murray), 41–42, 45,
  120
Carey, Fabian, xii, 2, 15–17,
  22n59, 117; death, 112, 118–19;
  as Director of Blackfriars Guild,
  73, 80–94, 99–104, 108–11,
  118, 122; Nagle and, 72–74; salary, 57; as set builder, organizer
  and fundraiser, 23–26, 30, 33,
  38–39, 45, 63, 70–74; as set de-

ABOUT THE AUTHOR

Matthew Donald Powell, O.P., a Catholic priest and a member of the Dominican Order, was born in Springfield, Ohio in 1943. He earned an M.A. in speech and theatre at Miami University (Ohio), an M.A. in theology at Aquinas Institute (Iowa) and a Ph.D. in theatre history and dramatic literature at the University of Wisconsin at Madison. Father Powell taught at Urbana University (Ohio) and Edgewood College (Wisconsin) before joining the faculty of Providence College (Rhode Island) in 1983. Since 1988 he has served as chairman of the Theatre Department at Providence.

Father Powell is also the author of *The Christmas Creche: A Treasure of Faith, Art, and Theatre* (Pauline Books and Media) and a dramatization of *The Canterville Ghost* (Meriwether Publishing/Contemporary Drama Service).